Rolling into the World

Packed with childhood adventures that are sometimes hilarious, sometimes terrible, *Rolling Into the World* begins with ABC broadcaster and former Federal MP Eoin Cameron's birth on the slopes of the volcanic crater of Mount Gambier. From riding on the lino polisher to homemade rocket launches, from Actavite to *Biggles*, his experiences growing up in a constantly expanding Catholic family during the 1950s and 60s make a terrific read.

Eoin Cameron was born in Mount Gambier in 1951, the second eldest of ten children. He worked as a farm labourer and roustabout in shearing teams in the Great Southern; did a stint in a salmon fishing team at Parry's Inlet and tried (unsuccessfully) to sell used cars in Albany. At eighteen he jagged a job as an announcer at Radio 6VA in Albany, where he met his wife Wendy. Eoin and his new family moved to Perth in the seventies, then Melbourne, then Perth again, to pursue his broadcasting career. In the nineties Eoin was elected the Federal Member for Stirling and served two terms in Canberra. Eoin is still married to Wendy and has three children and four grandchildren. He is currently breakfast presenter on ABC Local Radio in Perth.

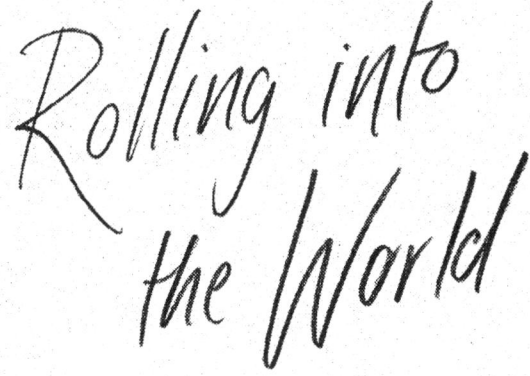

Rolling into the World

memoirs of a ratbag child

EOIN CAMERON

Fremantle Arts Centre Press

Australia's finest small publisher

This book is dedicated to my wife Wendy, who kept up the pressure to get it finished. To my parents Duncan and Imelda, who had the courage to 'seize the day' and head West with ten kids in tow. To Woz, Goog and Ig for their encouragement. To my cousin Rob and his family, and to Sister Andrina Foreman RSJ, born Margaret Foreman at Clare, South Australia, in 1929. She entered the convent at Kensington, South Australia in 1947. Sister Andrina dealt with 'ratbag' kids all over South Australia before she died at Tappeiner Court Nursing Home, Kensington in 1990. She was a great Tarantella dancer!

Acknowledgements

The photographs on pages 24, 29, 33, 145, 166 and 170 are reproduced with the kind permission of the City of Mount Gambier – Les Hill Photographic Collection of the Mount Gambier Public Library.

The photographs on pages 55 and 59 are reproduced with the kind permission of Our Lady of the Pines School, Nangwarry.

Contents

1

Jane Street

On the fourth day of January 1951, Communist forces overran the Korean capital Seoul in what was to be the early stages of a bitter and bloody war. At about the time that the Communist tanks were rolling into Seoul, I was rolling into the world in Mount Gambier, South Australia — well not exactly 'rolling' into the world. I'm sure my mother would have been mightily relieved had it been as easy as that, but in the sunrise hours of that summer day I was born in the beautiful old Mount Gambier hospital.

The hospital was set high on the slopes of the decaying craters of volcanoes long since dead, overlooking what was then a town of medium size, serving the timber milling and agricultural industries which lay around it. The old hospital was something of a gothic structure, which would have served well as the set for 'The Addams Family' or 'The Munsters' — grey and foreboding with turrets and spires, ramparts and balconies. The high-gloss green wards and dark corridors were probably hell to work in, because of their age, but the building was imposing, even lovely in its own way.

As we Australians tend to do to most of our structural heritage, the wreckers' ball found its way through the old building in 1971 after years of its standing vacant and falling into disrepair. The magnificent old hospital was replaced by an atrocity after the style of a Stalinist bunker, but then Stalinist bunkers were all the go in the fifties, and every hospital of the era must have been built from the same set of plans.

I was born second of ten kids to Duncan and Imelda. My folks met at a dance at the old Glencoe woolshed. My dad lived on a farm at Glencoe owned by his grandmother and uncle. His father was a stock and station agent I think, but he died just a few days after Mum and Dad married. Although we kids never knew either of our grandfathers, we referred to them as 'Papa' Cameron and 'Papa' Harrap respectively.

For Mum and Dad it must have been love at first sight, because Dad used to ride for miles on his pushbike from Glencoe into Mount Gambier when he was courting my mum in the late forties. Dad was a 'rev head' before 'rev heads' had been heard of, and after the bicycle he got a motorbike, and by the time I came along they'd progressed to a Morris Cowley.

Religion didn't take long to rear its ugly head. Mum was the youngest of twelve kids, Dad the eldest of seven. The Camerons were Presbyterian, the Harraps Catholic. This may have been the cause of some early family tensions, but as kids we were pretty much oblivious to anything that might have been bubbling away under the surface in family relationships. All our Harrap relatives were Catholic, and all the Camerons Protestant, except for one great uncle who married a Catholic girl, and brought their kids up as Catholics. In our case my mum won out too, because most of us ended up with Catholic names and, at least in the beginning, went to Catholic schools.

The best thing about being part of a large family is that you can seem to have literally millions of relatives. I had aunties and uncles coming out of my ears. Some people might see that as something of a setback, but growing up in a mid-sized country town, it was definitely a plus to be related to a large proportion of the population. For a start, it seemed that you knew someone in every second street, so 'Safety Houses' were unheard of and unnecessary. There were always plenty of cousins to muck around with, and some family or other would always be going to the beach or on a picnic with room for another child or two to tag along.

My older brother is Peter, then after me came Charles, Malcolm, Bernadette, Josephine, Gerard, Mary, Murray and Imelda. I suppose had there been more kids we would have surely included a Theresa, Clare, Damien or Patrick! My mother apparently wasn't overly thrilled with my arrival — in later years she confided she had desperately wanted a girl, having just had her first boy. But, there I was, unwanted or not; I was here to stay.

If she was hanging for a girl, Mum was in for a pretty tough old time. Disappointment was to follow disappointment with the arrival of Charles and then Malcolm. I'm sure she wouldn't have described their births that way, but the drought finally broke with the arrival of Bernadette.

Ignorance truly is bliss, and I didn't discover for many years the facts about my frosty reception — it's probably something that falls into the 'too much information' category — you don't really need to know you were rejected at birth. But it couldn't have scarred me too badly, because for all my life I've been under the impression I was a favourite. Of course, at some level I might have known, for once the thaw began, to pay my mother back, I promptly refused to breastfeed. Or this may have been nature's way of issuing an early warning: 'Don't push it, when this kid starts to eat he won't stop!' And I didn't! Although I was never obese, I was what might be called 'well covered', with a metabolism which was super efficient when it came to making the most of everything I ate.

* * * *

Not that I could have cared less at the time, but the big movies of the year of my birth have certainly stood the test of time. The Best Picture Oscar went to *An American In Paris*, which was some feat when you consider it was up against *The African Queen*, for which Humphrey Bogart got the gong as Best Actor, and *A Streetcar Named Desire* with Vivien Leigh as Best Actress. Interestingly 1951 was also the year of the introduction of colour television in the United States, though it would be more than twenty years before our TV screens burst into colour. Come to think of it, in 1951 we didn't even have black and white TV: we had to wait until the Melbourne Olympics in 1956 for that.

* * * *

Wanted or not, I was taken home from hospital to a little house in Jane Street. Jane Street ran parallel with Mount Gambier's main drag, Commercial Street, and the house was of the kind where the verandah meets the footpath. The house had been there so long, it looked like it was sinking into the ground, an impression confirmed by the limestone walls, which drew up the damp from the earth and were covered in moss and mould. The inside, too, was gloomy and dank and very basic. Life probably wasn't all that easy for my mum, with a succession of new babies, and such basic living conditions.

* * * *

The kitchen had an old zinc sink with a razor-sharp edge. When I was very small I stood on my three-wheeler to get some extra height to reach the tap. Of course, the trike rolled out from under me. I grabbed the sharp edge of the sink to prevent my fall, and badly slashed three of the fingers of my right hand almost through to the bone.

With older toddler (Peter) in tow and new baby (Charles) under her arm, Mum ran me around to the doctor's house, fortunately only a street away, to have me patched up. Maybe my fingers were too small, or perhaps I was carrying on too badly for him to even attempt to stitch me, but for whatever reason the doctor treated my fingers with some kind of powder and bandaging. Under the circumstances, he did a fairly good job, though to this day I'm left with an impressive set of scars and a little finger the nerves of which are well and truly buggered. Over the years I've managed to impress people with various stories explaining how I got the scars: just about any tale has to be more exciting than grabbing the sharp edge of a sink when a trike disappeared from under me.

I must have spent a lot of time naked in the backyard of Jane Street.
Here being hosed down by older brother Peter.

Au naturel again in the Jane Street backyard.

* * * *

The house in Jane Street had a large backyard with a timber fence surrounding it. We had a great time in summer playing under the sprinkler and making a glorious mess with mud pies. Where there's mud there's worms, and I think my mum took a long time to recover after putting her hand into the pocket of a pair of Peter's shorts one washing day, only to grab half a pound of plump and juicy wriggling earthworms.

We didn't see much of Dad at Jane Street. He'd be gone before daylight and wouldn't get home until after dark. At the time he was setting up a partnership with Uncle Allen, one of Mum's brothers, to mill timber. They had a single circular sawbench, belt-driven by an old tractor engine. I'm not sure how long they operated like that before they built their first 'proper' mill, but they must have been doing all right because before I started school, Mum and Dad built a brand new house in a 'new area' of town in Acacia Street.

Altogether, my recollections of the Jane Street house are fairly sparse, and I probably only remember it at all because for years after we'd left it, we'd be told 'that's where we used to live' every time we drove past.

* * * *

While our house was being built in Acacia Street, Princess Elizabeth became Queen upon the death of her father King George VI, Dwight D Eisenhower became President of the United States, Edmund Hillary and Tenzing Norgay climbed Mount Everest, Dr

Jonas Salk began innoculating children against polio, and Rock and Roll was sweeping the world. American disc jockey Allen Freed had used the term 'Rock and Roll' to describe the rhythm and blues music which up until the early fifties had mainly been popular with black Americans. Somehow the expression 'Rock and Roll' was more acceptable to white society. Bill Haley and the Comets were unlikely Rock and Roll idols — Bill was overweight with thinning hair, and the group looked like a collection of middle-class accountants — but 'Shake Rattle and Roll' they did, and hit the charts. Critics of the day wrote it off as a passing fad, but Rock and Roll was here to stay.

Grace Kelly was the darling of the big screen, she picked up the Best Actress Oscar in 1954 for *The Country Girl*, and the brooding and edgy Marlon Brando was Best Actor in the Oscar-winning movie of the year, *On The Waterfront*.

* * * *

Things must have been going fairly well at the mill, and quite a number of my relatives, mainly uncles, were working with my dad and Uncle Allen, and it wasn't long before we shifted to Acacia Street. The new area of town was full of streets called Banksia, Wattle, Redgum and so on; it was a veritable forest, with not a tree in sight.

Dad had managed the building of the house himself, organising the various tradesmen. Like most houses at that time, it was built from Mount Gambier stone, huge ashlars of sawn limestone. In the stone you could see all the little seashells and fossilised bits of creatures from ancient times. Mount Gambier stone made an excellent building material because the blocks were so thick, about six inches. They made terrific insulation in summer, but were not so marvellous in winter when they always seemed a bit damp and cold.

If you didn't whitewash the house fairly regularly, it became discoloured with the damp into a dull blotchy grey colour. Even if the damp didn't extend to the interior, it looked miserable, so it was a regular ritual to paint the house with 'Boncote' to keep it bright and white. Contrast the white walls with bright blue gutters and rich red corrugated iron roof, and in the parlance of the time our new house was 'snazzy' to say the least!

Leading down from our back porch was a concrete ramp, and as we went down the ramp and around the corner of the house, we kids would often take a bite out of the edge of the limestone, chew it and spit it out. It made your teeth go all slippery and squeaky. Dad wasn't all that impressed. He'd say to Mum, 'You wouldn't believe it, but those little b's are slowly eating the house!' Dad didn't use the 'f' word in those days, but of course those were the days before he was truly tested, although the kids slowly eating the house should have given him a rough pointer as to what he could expect.

All our relatives and friends oohed and aahed over our new house, and it truly must have been a picture in a 1950s sort of way. The kitchen was a big room with a Rayburn slow combustion stove. There were overhead cupboards as well as under bench cupboards, and each cupboard door was painted a different colour. Vinyl floor tiles were laid in a random pattern, again in every colour under the sun, and some colours, I'm sure, which didn't occur naturally. They were very classy tiles, with flecks through them to give a sort of marbled effect, and to keep them in peak condition, they had to be polished once Mum had washed them. Being resourceful, which was probably a matter of necessity, Mum would spread the Wundawax over the tiles, then let us kids slide all over them in thick socks. We also had a state of the art maroon and silver electric polisher, which looked like a cross between the front bonnet of an FJ Holden and a Second World War German helmet. It had three rotating polishing brushes and was virtually uncontrollable at any speed. If the polisher actually physically got away from you, the motor would automatically cut out as soon as the handle hit the floor. Which was good to know. Bernadette being the baby at the time would get to ride on the polisher as it whirred around, although Mum wasn't too keen on that idea. 'You could hit a wet patch,' she used to say, 'and the baby could be electrocuted.' I think what she was really worried about was the baby weeing into the polisher's motor, and getting electrocuted in that way.

In the centre of the kitchen stood our chrome and Laminex table and chairs. The top of the table was green fake marble and the chairs were padded with green vinyl with cream piping — the height of good taste, though I don't know why the chairs weren't all in different colours, to go along with the cupboard doors and floor tiles.

Off the kitchen was the dining room, except we hardly ever ate in there. The phone was in the dining room. It was the black Bakelite type with a rotary winder knob on the front of it and the bell fixed to the wall, separate from the phone. It had a particularly loud ring, and could be heard all over the house. The phone itself could be unplugged from the wall socket quite easily, and often proved an irresistible target for young hands. On one of the numerous occasions when the phone had disappeared and the bell was ringing off the wall, Mum was dashing around screeching, 'Where's the ruddy phone?' — 'Ruddy' was about as profane as Mum got — and Charles, the toddler at the time, was kneeling down by the empty phone socket, yelling, 'Hang on, Mum's coming!'

Between the dining room and lounge, and the lounge and the entry hall, there were double glass doors etched with mermaids blowing bubbles. Now we're talking 'real snazzy' — the mermaids had breasts. As breast feeding was an ongoing feature in our house, the mermaids' breasts were not particularly fascinating until we noticed that the kids of visiting friends and relatives were transfixed by them, with lots of giggling and snickering about 'rude bits'.

* * * *

Because our house was fairly big for the time, Mum and Dad used to hold 'Housie' nights to raise funds for the church and for Mater Christi, the Catholic school — Housie was a game a lot like Bingo, if not the same. It was at one of these Housie nights, when sleeping arrangements had been changed about, that things went terribly wrong. Some people would bring their kids with them, and put them down to sleep in the big kids' bedroom, which was more like a dormitory with four beds in it. This was the room we four eldest boys usually slept in, but for the purposes of the evening, we were all put in Mum and Dad's bed.

Exploring Mum and Dad's room was pretty exciting at any time, and this particular night was no exception. There was nothing spectacular to report, except that in the top drawer of the laminated cherry wood dressing table with its circular scallop-edged mirror, there was a box of Aspros. Aspros were mysterious things that grown-ups took from time to time to make them feel better. They were packaged in a fascinating way, with all the little tablets folded neatly inside what was effectively a long paper tape. Aspros then tasted much as they do now — pretty dreadful — but what's a kid to do? I ate the lot! This was just before I started school, so I must have been about four at the time, and I should have known better, especially considering the Aspros tasted so horrible.

I don't recall whether the downhill slide was sudden and I certainly don't recall what brought my overdose to the attention of the adults — probably one of my brothers dobbed me in — but that was the ruin of one perfectly good Housie night. The family doctor, whom I believe secretly loathed us kids, told my mum over the phone to make me drink heaps of warm salty water. I don't know how much salty water was forced down my throat but it seemed like gallons, and it had the desired effect — the entire contents of my stomach, including the Aspros and probably one or two of my lesser organs, presented themselves into the bucket that had been strategically placed in front of me. I don't know exactly what part my Aunty Ev played in this little saga, but she must have had something to do with it, because to this day, whenever I think of Aunty Ev, I can taste Aspros and warm salty water.

About this time, Josephine made her appearance. At last another girl, and a sister for Bernadette. We called her Fluff because of her fluffy hair and the name stuck.

2

The Odeon

Mount Gambier in the fifties had two picture theatres, the King's and the Odeon. The King's Theatre was for more serious business, travelling shows and plays and so on; the Odeon was the more popular by far, and tended to have the best movies, or pictures as we called them then, especially as far as kids were concerned. The Odeon was a picture theatre in the grand old chintzy style, with huge red velvet curtains with gold tassel trimmings, and ornate ceilings and cornices. You could sit upstairs, downstairs or in the 'lovers seats'. The lovers seats were really two seater lounges that always seemed to be taken by bodgies snogging their girlfriends (called widgies), who usually weren't the remotest bit interested in what was going on on the screen, they were only there to snog. Bodgies and widgies were older than us, at least sixteen, some maybe up to twenty years old. The boys wore tight jeans with a leather piece above the back pocket, often with their name, or their girlfriend's name burnt into the leather with a hot iron. Their shirts were in really bright colours with the collars turned up, and if they were the 'real article' they had leather jackets with metal studs. The girls wore tight blouses with black stretchy pants; they had 'big' hair, and you couldn't tell what they really looked like because of the amount of make-up they trowelled on. And they all smoked. Fortunately the bodgies and widgies mainly went to the pictures at night.

The Odeon must have had fairly creative management because certain sessions were dedicated to particular types of movies, for instance there was 'Romance' night, which you wouldn't be seen dead at. Thursday night was 'Ranch' night, when they'd feature two cowboy movies. We were never allowed to go to ranch nights, because there was school the next day. I swore that when I grew up I'd go to every one. In fact I think I only ever went to one ranch night, and didn't enjoy it all that much. I hated the way the cowboys always won.

The day of the week we lived for was Saturday. The Saturday pictures — the Matinee as it was called — had a main feature, a support film, and of course the serial. Because of the large number of kids in our family and extended family, there were always plenty of people to go to with. My cousin Robin was my best mate, and he loved the pictures as much as I did, even though he was always on the cowboys' side. From when I was about ten, his dad or my dad would drop us off at the Odeon with two bob each, which we considered a fortune. The Saturday Matinee cost 1/3d downstairs and 1/6d upstairs. Mum always told us we had to go upstairs so as not to hang around with the 'tough' kids downstairs. I'm not sure why Mum thought her kids were any less 'tough' than any of the other Mount Gambier variety, but that's how it was. Needless to say

The Odeon picture theatre.

we went downstairs. The extra threepence could buy a hell of a lot of rotgut lollies in those days. On the way out we'd rummage through the bins to get some upstairs ticket butts in case the folks asked us where we sat. Explaining minor injuries was trickier, but that's the risk you run hanging around with 'tough' kids. One Saturday, a kid fell from the upstairs balcony onto the seats below. God knows how he did it, but apart from being badly winded he was otherwise uninjured — we were extremely impressed!

The lollies they sold at the Odeon were a lot more expensive than anywhere else in town — nothing has changed much over the years in that regard. Our favourites when we could afford them were Jaffas, great for rolling around the theatre once the lights went down. You could use the orange outer shell as a 'lipstick' by wiping it all over your wet lips. Choo Choo bars were great, but made your mouth and teeth blue or black — decisions, decisions. Fantales with stories about Doris Day and Sophia Loren and Rock Hudson before he was gay, Jersey Toffees, and yard long licorice strips called Black Boy with a picture of what we in our political naivety called a 'black sambo' on the front. There was Fanta and Coke to slosh it all down with, and choc-ices if you had enough dosh left. The choc-ices could be a bit dodgy though. They came in a blue and silver wrapper, and the chocolate was very thin. Unless you gutsed them down very quickly, you could end up with a hell of a mess.

The Queen would get the pictures under way. 'God Save the Queen' would strike up, and she would appear in a red jacket and fur cap on the back of a horse in what we took to be the front yard of Buckingham Palace. You could see her even before the curtains were pulled back, and she gradually became clearer as the screen was revealed. Everyone stood up as a mark of respect, except of course the toughs who whistled and made smart remarks and horse farting sounds. Any grown-ups who happened to brave the matinee would mutter darkly about how 'common' some kids were and how it was probably the 'new Australians' who didn't know any better.

The films were generally unremarkable. I can hardly put a name to any of them, mostly churned-out Hollywood 'B' grade flicks. But we really liked the war pictures, where week after week the Americans would save the world from whichever group of baddies were about to do us all over. The support films were even worse, usually old black and white things that held no one's attention. The noise level from the audience before intermission attested to this. The best part of the matinees were the serials, that we were all waiting for. They were saved for the end, and were obviously designed to get you back into the theatre the next week, as they invariably did. It didn't matter how dated or corny they were — we loved 'em! Batman was my favourite. However perilous the situation, you just knew that Batman and Robin would find a way out next week. My cousin Robin loved the fact that he had the same name as a super hero ... and I thought it was just a shame there were no screen heroes called Eoin.

I don't know why I always sided with the Indians — it certainly didn't have anything to do with political correctness. In Hollywood the Indians were *always* the baddies — low down, scheming, murdering savages — but I loved 'em. One year Mum and Dad made a trip to Melbourne around Christmas time and brought us all back special presents. I got an Indian outfit and if I'd died then I would have died completely happy! It was beige in colour with a loose top and long trousers and different coloured fringed bits around the edges. I don't suppose any tribe that ever existed wore anything remotely like my Indian suit, but I couldn't have cared less. And the climate of Mount Gambier being what it is, even the bravest Sioux or Apache would probably have agreed that long trousers were preferable to a lap-lap. Only the headdress didn't overly impress me: there were just half a dozen different coloured feathers, altogether too scrawny and unimpressive for any dinky-di brave to be seen dead in.

I managed to augment the scungy headdress with chook

feathers, and made a truly spectacular war bonnet. The brown and orange feathers from the darker chooks were okay as they were, but the white feathers from the leghorns had to be dealt with. I coloured them with 'Blue-O' from Aunty Elvie's laundry. I'm sure that Sitting Bull or Crazy Horse wouldn't have worn pale blue feathers, but I didn't care, I thought I looked pretty good. After I'd done all the secret Indian rituals and painted myself up with some of Mum's or Aunty Iris's lipstick that I'd pinched, I could go on the warpath for hours, attacking anything that moved — mainly dogs and cats — with my bow and rubber suction cup tipped arrows.

Robin always had really cool cowboy stuff, plastic 'wrangler' pants, six-shooters in holsters, cowboy hat; you name it, he had it. His mum and dad — Aunty Iris and Uncle Glen — spoiled him rotten. His six shooters would take rolls of caps, and you could blast away for hours, by which time all the domestic animals within two blocks had gone into hiding.

Robin was also really clever at making things, and he made some brilliant bows and arrows. He'd make the arrows from the tongue part of tongue-and-groove floorboards that were manufactured at a nearby mill. He'd sharpen the sliver of wood up, stick some chook feathers in the blunt end, and away you'd go. One afternoon our Apache war party was lying in ambush under the privet hedge along the front of our house, when a Paleface, in the form of Robin's sister Cheryl, came into sight. We launched our surprise attack. Two arrows shot gracefully through the air, mine landing with a thud about three feet away from the Paleface. Robin, being a dramatically better shot, had more success. His arrow lodged between her left eyeball and lower eyelid. King Harold at the Battle of Hastings had nothing on Cheryl's performance. She belted inside screaming like a banshee, not surprisingly. Mum managed to remove the arrow without fainting and, miraculously, there was no damage to Cheryl's eye. It goes without saying that bows and arrows were henceforth banished, at least when grown-ups were snooping around. We kept a secret cache in our fort in the stinkweed on the vacant block up the road, just on the off-chance some evil dudes might be marauding the open plains, mesas and gulches of Acacia Street.

* * * *

Considering the fairly hectic breeding cycle going on at our house, Mum and Dad always seemed to have a pretty busy social life. We always had friends and rellies calling around, or we'd be visiting them. For a while they also went out to the pictures on Friday nights. When I was seven or eight they took a couple of us older kids with them, probably to ease the burden on the babysitter. That's how I saw *A Town Like Alice*. The story itself probably didn't interest me one bit, except for the action bits, but one scene scared the living daylights out of me. It was the part where all the kids had to hide under their desks from the Japanese soldiers. For weeks after that I'd keep looking out the windows at school just in case soldiers in tropical uniform were sweeping in off Penola Road to storm the walls of Mater Christi. As far as I can remember, Mum and Dad didn't take us to the pictures at night again, until the drive-in came along.

Mount Gambier is built on the slopes and rich volcanic soil plains surrounding the craters of extinct volcanoes. Within the

Mount Gambier with Browne's Lake to the right and Valley Lake in the foreground.

craters are the famous Blue Lake from which the district draws its water supply, and the lesser known Valley, Browne's and Leg of Mutton lakes. The Mount is about a fifteen minute drive to the coast and the town of Port MacDonnell, 'the Bay' as the locals call it. The Bay is an unremarkable town but was a source of great adventure for me in the fifties. Robin was the only boy in his family, and I was his best mate, so I was often included in their holidays and weekends away. Aunty Iris and Uncle Glen Howell, or 'Codger' as my dad called him, would often camp out at the Bay, and we'd muck around in the seaweedy water, marvelling at the phosphorescence of what we called 'sea lice'. They'd glow in the

With my cousin Robin in the backyard of his house in Shelton Street.

dark, and you could wipe them up and down your arms and become a human beacon, years before the French had started making the Pacific glow.

Summer at the Bay was great, we'd scoff down 'rockets' — frozen blue cordial on a stick in the shape of a rocket. God only knows what they were coloured with. Robin's folks had a forties Chevrolet Fleetmaster. It was a huge blue thing with acres of room inside and rear doors that opened the wrong way, towards the back. After a big day at the Bay, the trip home to the Mount seemed to take forever. We'd be huddled under the tartan travelling rug which was a feature of the back shelf of every car in those days, invariably sunburnt with skin like sandpaper. Sometimes we'd stop and pick up supper at the Blue Lake Fish Supply in Commercial Street. Supper consisted of Coca Cola and potato cakes — slices of potato dipped in batter and deep fried, absolutely delicious — cholesterol hadn't been heard of then. The Blue Lake Fish Shop had streams of water running down its front window. I thought that was the height of sophistication.

* * * *

Along with all his other cool gear, Robin had a collection of plastic toys that he'd more or less grown out of. You can imagine the stuff: plastic tip trucks, cars, boats and so on. We were very fond of fire — possibly almost to the extent of pyromania. Sometimes Aunty Iris would let us build a camp fire in their backyard, as long as we were 'careful'. This particular day, we borrowed one of Aunty Iris's larger saucepans and decided to melt down all of the unwanted plastic toys. One by one we loaded the toys into the saucepan, fishing out the metal bits with a stick as the plastic melted down. It was fantastic, the smell was toxically overpowering and we ended up with a seething pot of multicoloured goo pouring off clouds of black smoke. Unfortunately the smoke attracted the attention of Robin's folks. Before they could do much, however, the plastic lava burst into flame, and burnt itself and the saucepan into a twisted mess. It was one of the few times I ever saw Robin's parents completely lose it — I thought that was something that only happened at my place.

* * * *

My maternal grandmother, Mama Harrap, lived with us quite a lot and she had a room of her own at Acacia Street. I don't know what it was in particular about her green candlewick double bedspread, but it featured in a couple of minor disasters. Before Mum and Dad would go out to the pictures on Friday nights, we all had to be in bed. Of course the moment the car had pulled out of the driveway, we'd be straight out of bed. Mama would spoil us rotten and let us run amok. She was an elderly lady but she was totally switched on and she'd clean up all evidence of our carryings on before the folks got home. Frankly, I'm sure they guessed a bit of what was going on, but turned a blind eye just to get a few hours peace each week. Some nights we'd drag the bedspread off Mama's bed and lay it over the kitchen table. The bedspread would almost reach the floor on all sides, making a fantastic hide-out in which we'd carry out the craze of the week. Sometimes we'd glue pop sticks together to make

There was great excitement when the Queen visited Mount Gambier in 1954.
The whole town was awash with flags. Mum and Dad took us to a good
vantage point near the main street and Dad sat me on his shoulders as the
procession of black cars drove by. Peter and I each had a little Union Jack.

miniature forts; sometimes we'd play with Dad's torch until the
battery was flat; other times we'd glue ourselves and everything else
to the floor cutting and pasting.

One fateful night we were in our hide-out cutting stuff out of
magazines with Mama's dressmaking scissors. I don't know why he
did it — why do kids do anything? — but my brother Peter cut off
the end of his tongue with the pinking shears. Actually he didn't cut
it completely off, but near as well as, it was hanging from a bit of

gristle on one side — not that you could see it all that clearly, because he was squealing like a stuck pig, with gallons of blood pouring out of his mouth. The rest of that night was a bit of a blur. I was, no doubt, unceremoniously shoved back to bed; I think my parents' names were put up on the screen at the pictures. The doctor got involved, there were stitches, and quite a degree of unpleasantness between my mother and her mother: 'What were the ruddy kids doing out of bed, under the table draped in a double bedspread, playing with scissors in the first place?'

* * * *

I started school at Mater Christi College in 1956, the year the Olympic games and television came to Australia. I was hardly aware of either, perhaps because the trauma of starting school had my undivided attention. Mater Christi was run by the Mercy nuns. They were traditional nuns in full drag — black and white, long habits and veils. My grade one teacher was Sister Clare. Like most nuns, she was of indeterminate age with a happy red face — a bit like an embarrassed penguin. Like a lot of the other kids I howled on my first day at school. There was none of that acclimatising rubbish with kids spending a few hours a day at school for a few weeks to get used to it — no siree, it was the sharp 'snap' of Mum's apron strings, and in at the deep end. Sister Clare was very sweet. One day after I knocked myself out cold on the ice-clad puddles on the tennis court, she wrapped me in a blanket and sat me in front of the open fire in our classroom. I really dragged out my recovery.

These were the days of Dick and Dora and Nip and Fluff, and we even had an elocution teacher who came in once a week to try to teach us to talk proper. I couldn't quite grasp why we had to keep saying 'how now brown cow' over and over, with our little lips supposedly forming a perfect 'o'.

Grade two was a different story. Sister Carmel was just as sweet as Sister Clare, but through her years of teaching six- and seven-year-olds she knew every scam in the book, and it took her approximately ten seconds to suss out me and my cousin Robin. In grade two I had my mouth washed out with soap for using 'filthy' language. I'd made the mistake of telling a kid he was a 'poo-face' at recess. I was dobbed on immediately and had to confess that 'Yes indeed' I had been using filthy language and gutter talk. I'm only glad I didn't know the 'f' word at the time, God only knows what my fate might have been — although I suspect Sister Carmel probably didn't know that word either.

As I said, the advantages of growing up in a country town outweigh the disadvantages many times over, especially with such a large extended family. Our house was about a mile from the school, and on the way home there were always one or two stop-offs, usually at Aunty Elvie's for sandwiches (Vegemite or jam) and drop scones or rock cakes, depending on what was hot out of the oven that particular day. In winter it was hot sweet cocoa, and in summer Fifty Fifty Kia-Ora cordial straight out of the Kelvinator.

Aunty Elvie was my mum's eldest sister and she was married to Uncle Jack. Their house was very old and very close to the footpath in Wyatt Street. It had a long central passageway with rooms off each side and the kitchen at the back. The kitchen had

First Communion day with brothers Peter and Charles.

an old-fashioned Metters wood stove, and on the mantelpiece there was a line-up of pressed tin canisters, featuring pictures of Australian wildlife, for tea, coffee, sugar and so on. At the very back of the house was a lean-to where Aunty Elvie had her laundry, basically a set of cement troughs and a built-in copper. She used to boil up the washing in the copper, stirring it around with a broomstick. There were always bags of Blue-O for brightening up the whites.

There were always visitor too at Aunty Elvie's, especially on Fridays, when everyone seemed to do their shopping. If visitors were in evidence, we'd listen at the door to see if we could identify who was there before we went in. If we heard Aunty Jean's voice we'd pass on the snack for the day. Aunty Jean always had a disapproving air about her. However, Aunty Elvie and Uncle Jack had a huge 'Lassie' dog, a collie called Pal, who would give away our presence with his deep resonant woof. Pal used to insist upon 'shaking hands' by raising his paw until you shook it. He was a beautiful old dog, with the patience of Job.

My Uncle Jack had a big overstuffed easy chair by the fire in the kitchen, where he used to sit reading. He didn't say a lot; he probably never had the chance to get a word in anyway. Uncle Jack had a magnificent vegetable garden at one side of the house and he used to grow everything under the sun in the rich volcanic soil. A highlight of the year was the arrival of his 'new' potatoes, usually just in time for Christmas. What a treat — boiled new potatoes with fresh mint, pepper and salt, and lashings of butter. Uncle Jack's rhubarb we weren't so wild about, but the new potatoes certainly made up for that.

Uncle Jack's brother 'Uncle Alf' and his mate 'Uncle Jimmy' lived next door to us in Acacia Street. They weren't really uncles, but in those days any adult friends of Mum and Dad's were Uncle or Aunty to us. Alf and Jimmy were great gardeners too, and used to win prizes at the show for their 'gladdies'. They used to trap rabbits to make money, and had a shed full of rabbit skins stretched over wire to dry. Because they'd lived through the Depression they were extremely resourceful, and it seemed to me they could turn their hand to just about anything.

* * * *

There was a nasty incident at Mater Christi which turned me off braces for life, even on the occasions when they have been fashionable. In 1956 braces were de rigueur to hold up the grey melange school shorts. They were also hell to get out of in a hurry, especially when you'd left it too late mucking around at recess time. Recess was only fifteen minutes, so you had to get an awful lot done in a very short time. Drinking milk was compulsory. The government provided the milk free, in tiny bottles with foil tops. It was okay in winter when the weather would keep the bottles cold, but in the warmer weather, the milk would get pretty gross with the cream congealing on the top. By the time you'd downed your government issue milk and stuffed down a slice of Mum's American Beauty rainbow cake — or whatever else White Wings were promoting at the time — there was only about ten minutes mucking around time left, bearing in mind a visit to the toilet also had to be managed. Time was tight to say the least. This particular day, I'd allowed approximately sixty seconds to do 'number twos', and unfortunately it took me all of that time just to get the braces undone ... and so the 'nest was filled'. I skipped the rest of the day and made the longest walk home in my life. I must have looked like a miniature bandy-legged stockman.

* * * *

While I was at Mater Christi I trained to be an altar boy. The training was done by an old nun called Sister Margaret. She was a large woman, not tall, but with an impressive circumference. She was also a bit of a character and smelled like she carried camphor balls around in her voluminous pockets. Most importantly, she had a jar full of jelly babies to use as bribes or rewards for her music or Latin students. I picked up the Latin Mass really quickly, probably because I loved the jelly babies, although I didn't have the remotest idea what the words meant. I learned them like a parrot. I have to say, the Mass sounded far more interesting in Latin — when the reforms came and the Mass was said in English, I found out that the exotic words I'd been parroting were quite dull.

My career as an altar boy continued until I left school, and it probably gave me my first taste of theatrics. I loved it. The dressing up, the pomp, the crowds, the smell of the incense. No one could ring a bell, bang a gong or swing an incense burner with quite my aplomb, and besides there were the occasional windfalls which came with the job. Because of my endless supply of older cousins, there were plenty of weddings with nuptial Masses. Weddings were always held on Saturdays, on which day there wasn't a line of altar boys keen to 'frock up' and do an extra Mass or two. The going rate was about ten bob, to be paid by the groom. Ten shillings was a smallish fortune at the time, so as far as I was concerned the more family weddings there were the better, and besides, you got to go to the reception and gorge yourself on as much cake and cool drink as you could handle.

3

Space and the Spacemaster

At seven o'clock each night, Mum and Dad would tune in to the ABC news on the wireless. If we kept dead quiet, we might be able to stay up a few minutes longer, but one peep out of us, and it was off to bed, no questions asked. It seemed from the news that bombs were going off all over the place — the Americans were testing the H-bomb at Bikini Atoll. Dad said the 'Yanks' had to keep ahead of the Russians, because if there was another war, it would be the end of all of us, and nothing could survive on earth after an all-out atomic war.

The Russians were doing really well in what was being called the Space Race. In 1957, when they launched Sputnik, we were all agog. One night, perched on the wooden fence between our place and Garrards, the next-door neighbours, Dad pointed out Sputnik to us. It looked like any other star in the sky, but it *moved*, and I'll never forget it. I think all of Australia was looking skywards that night.

When the Russians sent a dog into space later the same year, I was truly impressed. I'd seen the first Sputnik, and now to think a dog was up there in space aboard one was truly amazing. The

Russian dog was called Laika, and suddenly he was the most famous dog in the world. I started asking my dad awkward questions like, 'How long is Laika going to stay in space?' I was truly horrified when Dad told me Laika would stay there forever, that he would just 'go to sleep' when the air ran out, which would be in a few days at most. At night in bed all I could think was, what if it were my Wallaroo up there all lonely in space. I could only hope that Laika had plenty of lollies and biscuits with him until he went to sleep. Laika's fate just helped underline to me all the shocking things I'd been hearing about the 'Communists'. If they could do something so dreadful to a lovely dog like Laika, what wouldn't they do if they managed to get their evil hands on a Catholic kid!

Our dog Wallaroo was named after the town he came from about a hundred and fifty kilometres north-west of Adelaide. I'm not sure what sort of dog he was, probably a 'bitser', but they told us he was an Australian terrier. He was very long suffering; he had to be, I suppose, in a family with so many kids to torment him. He was not good with roads or motor vehicles, and seemed to be constantly getting run over to varying degrees, right up until the *big* one! Some dogs just don't learn, and Wallaroo never did — he'd just get excited and run after trucks, cars, motorbikes, you name it. In retrospect, Wallaroo was not what you might describe as a handsome dog, but he did have character, and we liked him. He also had mange. Mum said he only had mange because of all the 'rotgut' we fed him — cakes, biscuits and lollies — and it wasn't natural for dogs to eat that stuff. The way Wallaroo wolfed all the rotgut down, he obviously thought it was natural enough. Tic-Tocs were his favourite, and he'd spend ages licking the icing off before gulping down the biscuit clock face.

Every milk bar (as delis used to be called) sold little cellophane bags of sherbet with a licorice straw poking out the top. After you sucked out most of the sherbet and ate the straw, it was great to rip open the packet and let Wallaroo go for it. He'd stick his nose in and lick like mad. Of course some of the sherbet would get up his nose and set off a sneezing fit. We'd be falling about laughing while Wallaroo sneezed and bubbled away, but it must have been worth the trouble, because he always came back for more.

* * * *

While we were in Acacia Street, Dad bought the Vanguard. To give it its full name, Vanguard Spacemaster, made by the British Standard Motor Company. It was black with a rounded back, so it looked a bit like a slater which had been pushed in at both ends. The seats had woven plastic covers in a red tartan design — it was snazzy. There was only one problem with the Vanguard: it wasn't very good in wet weather, and Mount Gambier is wet a lot of the time. Going through puddles of any size at all literally guaranteed it would conk out, causing Dad to mutter vulgar things.

In the fifties it was the fashion for garages to be separate from the house, and ours was no exception. We had a limestone garage at the end of the driveway, set back just slightly from the rear wall of the house. At the back of the garage was a sort of workshop area with a board on the back wall painted with the shapes of the various tools which were supposed to hang there — spanners, wrenches, saws and so on. I never recalled seeing the board complete with its full complement, probably because we kids 'borrowed' stuff from time to time, never to be seen again. Also at the back of the garage were some fitted shelves, filled with rows of paint tins containing the dregs of paint from various projects over the years.

One Saturday afternoon, Robin and I prised open an old tin of high gloss white paint, and for some reason decided it would be a good idea to paint our 'tags'. 'Tag' was the diminutive of 'taglet', which is what my mum called our penises. She said God gave us the taglet so that everyone could tell who were the boys and who were the girls. That seemed plausible enough. Anyway to cut a long story short, we painted our tags glossy white. It was quite effective really. Being a bit of an artist, I decided on the finishing touch. We wandered across the road, sans trousers, to a vacant block and picked what we used to call dandelions. These weren't true dandelions at all, but the flower of the common capeweed. We used to thread the flowers together and make chains to drape around our necks. Mum told us that wasn't such a good idea, because it would make us wet the bed. One of my cousins did in fact wet the bed after mucking around with dandelions, so of course the story had to be true. Bearing in mind I had approximately one million cousins, and no doubt all of them made a dandelion chain at some time or other, it's hardly surprising one of them subsequently wet the bed.

On this memorable day, Robin and I picked a dandelion each and poked the stem down the end of our glossy white tags. They looked very smart. We must have become bored with our creative little excursion fairly quickly, got dressed and continued whatever it was we were doing before the artistic flush hit us.

The sequel to this saga was played out around five o'clock that evening when it was time to go inside and get cleaned up. Bath time at our place was a fairly strategic exercise. With all the kids in our family, plus one or two 'ring ins', you had to have a plan. Little kids first, older ones last — bad luck if you got the last bath, because God knows what the other kids did in the water. There was also an up-side to the last bath — as each shift left, you added a little more hot water to warm it up, so the last ones had the deepest bath. This particular Saturday evening though, not even a woman as inured to unusual and surprising circumstances as my mum had become, could have imagined what was about to confront her *in stereo*.

When it came our turn, Robin and I stripped off and stood there, resplendent in white gloss and wilted dandelion. The paint had half dried and the dandelions looked as though they were there to stay. The look on Mum's face I'll never forget. She was truly speechless, and when eventually she could speak, she wasn't making any sense at all, just muttering, 'But how … why … what were you doing?' I thought it would have been pretty obvious what we'd been doing: we'd painted our penises and added a finishing touch, that's what we'd been doing.

Once again the dreaded family doctor got involved. I don't know exactly how Mum described the problem to him over the phone, but I'll bet he'd never encountered anything quite of this nature before. The sadistic mongrel suggested turps, a wise choice really, because after the turps had been administered we never again attempted anything even remotely approaching that level of creativity, at least where sensitive tissue was involved. Just in case you're wondering, for the roughly half the population who have testicles, just add a little dab of turps to the aforementioned bits — it's a sensation you're unlikely to forget. I'm sure that on that Saturday afternoon, if I'd known about the 'f' word, I would have used it!

I think our doctor's name was Robertson, and although our family must have provided him with a terrific amount of business, I'm sure he would have dreaded the sight of my mum or dad fronting up with any of us to his surgery. Because of the polio scare in those years, we got vaccinated for everything, and there was none of this namby-pamby oral vaccination — it was the syringe the size of a jackhammer variety — so naturally, a visit to the doctor's surgery for a 'jab' was a trauma-filled event for everyone. Doctor Robertson was not a young man, but reasonably fit, and he had to be. On one occasion he tried to coax me out from under the bed in his surgery with a jar of lollies. When he realised the futility of this, he climbed under the bed himself and wedged me in a corner to administer the shot. The only bright side of these traumatic visits was that he used plastic syringes and afterwards he'd break the needles off and let us take them home to use as water pistols.

* * * *

Our next door neighbours, the Garrards, were immaculate people. They had two boys. Their house was so tidy in contrast to the chaos of our household, I can remember being almost too nervous to go inside their door. Even the red painted back porch floor was polished, and shoes were lined up along the wall. No one walked inside with shoes on. The Garrards had a Vauxhall convertible, bright red with a cream canvas roof; it too was immaculate. I don't think I ever saw that car with the roof down. Convertibles were probably not designed for a climate like Mount Gambier's.

Further up our street, Mr and Mrs Graham had the most

incredible looking car, a grey Hudson. There weren't very many of them about, and the amazing thing about it was that the front looked almost the same as the back, so it was hard to tell if it was coming or going. The Grahams had a mechanical workshop where they did interesting things. Mum was always warning us not to go near the workshop because they did a lot of welding there. She said if we watched them welding without the proper goggles to protect our eyes we could get a 'flash'. A flash, we were told, was the most excruciating pain, like thousands of tiny razor blade cuts to your eyes, with salt thrown in for good measure. That of course was a challenge too good to miss, and Robin and I spent ages in the castor oil bushes across the road from Grahams Garage watching the welder as he arced up his rod. The fluorescent blue light and showers of sparks were spectacular, but as for the 'flash', disappointingly, nothing happened. We even went as far as watching through binoculars. Why we weren't blinded I don't understand.

* * * *

One afternoon in the late fifties something truly dreadful happened with the Vanguard. We were visiting my Aunty Phyllis and Uncle Allen — Dad's partner in the mill. The grown-ups were inside having afternoon tea, and my brothers and I were out the front impressing the Harrap girls. There were three of them, Maxine, Diane and Meredith. Meredith was about ten, Diane twelve and Maxine fourteen. I thought they were quite gorgeous as far as girls went, and they knew how to have a good time. We were lounging about in the Vanguard and the Harrap girls were standing chatting through the windows. For some reason unbeknownst to me, I put my finger in a small rip in the felt headlining of the car and made a slightly larger tear. 'Oh my God!' the girls yelled. 'You'll get killed for that!'

'We're not scared of Dad,' said one of my brothers, and with that made the rip a little larger. What followed was an appalling example of mob hysteria, and an early lesson on how things can swiftly get completely out of control. In approximately one minute we had demolished the interior of the Vanguard — head, seat and door linings shredded. What followed I don't remember precisely. I think it must have been so unpleasant my brain has blocked it all out. I do however have the distinct impression that this was the day I first heard the 'f' word, and I know for a fact the electric kettle cord was put to effective use the moment we got home. Amazingly, after such an incident, my parents went on to have a further five kids, which speaks volumes for their strength of character. The poor Vanguard never really recovered and fell further into disrepair.

* * * *

One time Dad came back from the city after a business trip with some crystal sets. He put up a wire aerial, strung along the outside of our house from our bedroom window across to the garage. I still don't know how they worked, but we'd lie in bed at night with our Bakelite headsets on, and listen to the radio. You could only pick up 5SE or 5MG, the local radio stations, but who cared? We'd listen to anything just for the novelty of it. Besides, it was our own radio, and we didn't have to listen to what Mum and Dad wanted to listen to on the mantelpiece radio in the kitchen.

Just north of Mount Gambier, at a place with the descriptive name of Dismal Swamp, Dad was growing some pines. One day he went out there to thin the pines, which you had to do to encourage upward rather than outward growth, and took Peter and myself with him. While Dad was working away, Peter and I were wrestling and rolling around on the ground, when I rolled onto a snake which bit me on the leg. Here we go again. Dad tied a tourniquet around my leg with some boot laces and put me in the back of the Vanguard. Unfortunately he'd only just started off when we hit a puddle and the car conked out. Luckily there was an old Second World War 'Blitz' truck in the forest, from Dad and Uncle Allen's mill. Because the truck had been stripped down for the purposes of log carting, it was really nothing more than a motor and a chassis, with a single seat for the driver. Dad tied me on the back of it and started to gun it, but got bogged within a few hundred yards. We were a fair way from the main road and I guess Dad was scared I'd snuff it before he could get help.

I first started thinking something must be really wrong when he picked me up and and began carrying me, running along the track through the forest with Peter tagging along behind. Dad was crying out loud, something I'd never seen, and frankly more alarming than the snakebite itself. Fortunately the Guardian Angels came to the rescue, in the form of some Italian people who were picnicking in the forest — something which was highly illegal because of the fire danger. The Italians had a Vanguard which didn't break down, and they soon had me at the Mount Gambier hospital where I was treated with antivenene for tiger snake bite — tiger snakes being extremely common in the swampy areas around the Mount. All I recall of the trip to hospital was wanting to go to sleep, and my dad and the Italian blokes trying desperately to keep me awake. The good side of all this was the presents I was showered with as I recovered in hospital.

4

Nangwarry

In the late fifties, when I was eight, we moved to a timber milling town called Nangwarry, about twenty minutes drive north of Mount Gambier on the road to Adelaide. We didn't live in the town itself, but a mile north, close to where Dad had a mill. Nangwarry was a government town of fibro houses, most of which were pretty near identical. The houses had been built for the mill workers. Most of the people in town had come to Australia after the war. There were Italians, Dutch, Scandinavians, Germans, Greeks, Croatians, you name it — Nangwarry was the original melting pot. Mostly people got along fairly well; just occasionally trouble would flare up between ethnic groups, very often between people of the same nationality. I remember there were dark mutterings about the 'Ustasha' influence in the town, and occasionally some skirmishes or a stabbing. Many of them were Catholics, and we spent more time with migrant kids than with the other kids in town, simply because we knew them from school.

Our house was virtually surrounded by pine plantations which stretched for miles in every direction and soon provided us with a source of revenue. Dad would pay us sixpence for every bag of pine cones we collected for the fire. The trouble was, the bags were old superphosphate bags, each of them about as tall as we were. After several days slaving to collect only a dozen bags of cones, we decided no more, there had to be easier ways to make some dosh.

The shortest way to school was along the pine break running parallel to the highway. The 'breaks' were all through the forests to assist with the management of the trees when they were young, and as protection against the ever-present threat of forest fire. Sometimes Mum would drive us to school, but we usually walked home. We had black plastic raincoats and sou'wester hats to protect us from the elements, but our shoes got into a shocking mess trudging along the breaks, especially if they had been recently ploughed. In spring everything was covered in pollen, it would even leave yellow scum floating in the swamps. Cockatoos would swarm all over the trees, looking for pine nuts, which of course were in endless supply.

The Nangwarry house was on a couple of acres with a really huge front lawn out to the highway. The house was built of weatherboard and fibro, and had an attic bedroom which we thought was fantastic, although it was like an oven up there in the summer months. It got so hot that the paint blistered off the banister on the stairs. Mum had the place redecorated with multi-coloured tiles in the kitchen — they were still fashionable — and this time again complemented them with cupboard doors each painted a different colour. There was Axminster carpet laid through all the living areas, the type with all the little grooves in it, which showed up every last skerrick of dirt or lint.

The most wonderful thing about the house, at least as far as I was concerned, was the bar under the stairs. Part of the counter lifted up to give access to the back of the bar, and we'd use it to play 'shops' and 'offices'. I doubt it was ever used for its real purpose, because the folks didn't drink much. Maybe some large brown bottles of beer at Christmas time, with a shandy for Mum, or perhaps a portergaff if she was pregnant, to help build up her iron.

The bathroom was really unusual for its time in that it was lined with varnished pine boards and always smelled like a forest. When it was steamy, the smell of the pine was particularly strong, sort of like a sauna in the days before we knew what a sauna was. Dad would stand us in front of the bathroom mirror each Sunday before Mass and 'Brylcreem' us. He'd slap the white muck on to his hands, rub them together and then slather it all over our heads whilst singing the Brylcreem song, 'Brylcreeeeem, a little dab'll do ya!' That was the genesis of my greasy hair phobia.

When Mama Harrap came to stay she had a room at the front of the house, at the foot of the stairs. Of course her bed was spread with the infamous green candlewick cover. One weekend when Robin came out to stay, I asked Mama if we could borrow her bedspread. She was a woman of great trust, and said, 'Okay, but just make sure your mother doesn't see it, or there'll be all kinds of bother,' and passed the bedspread out through her front window so we wouldn't be noticed. Robin and I took it to the mill yard next door where the sawn timber was neatly stacked in piles about twelve feet high. We intended using the bedspread as a parachute, not realising of course that candlewick is not silk, and twelve feet is not an ideal parachuting height. Holding two corners each, Robin and I didn't hesitate, over the side we went.

The following minutes were a bit of a blur — I lost two teeth and had extensive bruising; Robin bit his tongue very badly and split his bottom lip. He was also badly winded and lay sprawled on the ground making gurgling sounds with blood bubbling out of his mouth. After first aid from Mum, Robin was sent home to the Mount. I came out rather worse off with a really good tongue-lashing and threats about what was going to happen to me 'when your father gets home'. Mama Harrap really got the brunt of it, being reminded that someone of her age should know better etcetera etcetera. Mama just folded up the bloodied bedspread and retreated to her room.

* * * *

One Saturday afternoon a 'swaggie' called in. My mum gave him a billy of tea and sandwiches and off he went. Every few months he'd call in again on his way to wherever he was going. He was the first Aboriginal person I ever saw. I think Mum knew him; he had been fostered by a family in Mount Gambier, and he had attended the same primary school she went to. Until I was fifteen, and my family was on its way to Western Australia, I never saw another Aboriginal person. We learned about them at school, almost as if they no longer existed.

* * * *

Our Lady of the Pines opened in 1954,
with classes conducted in the local church.

When we first arrived at Nangwarry, school was in a church. Grades one, two and three desks were set up one behind the other in three rows in one half of the church, and behind a folding wooden partition were grades four, five, six and seven in four rows. Sister Florence and Sister Anthony were our teachers. They were 'Brown Joeys' — Josephite nuns of the order founded by Mother Mary MacKillop. The Joeys had quite a strong link with the south-east of South Australia, because Mary MacKillop had set up her first school at Penola, just a quarter of an hour up the road from Nangwarry. There were only minor differences in the way the

Josephites and the Mercy nuns looked, but they were worlds apart in attitude and philosophy. The Joeys who taught me were among the most down to earth women I've ever met.

Sister Florence was a fearsome old bat, and I didn't warm to her at all. I think she must have been past retirement age, and it showed. My first day in her class didn't help either, as she must have thought I was some kind of dimwit. In the grade four row there was a vacant seat alongside a kid who looked vaguely familiar, and turned out to be my second cousin Damien. Sister Florence (probably as a kindness) took me to the vacant seat and said, 'Damien, this is your cousin Eoin,' — to which he replied, 'No it's not.' He didn't know me from Adam, nor I him. We probably had seen each other before at some family 'do', but I certainly didn't recognise him, and the familiarity I sensed when I first laid eyes on him probably stemmed from the fact he looked more like me than my own brothers did. Despite this shaky start, we went on to become firm partners in crime.

Probably fortunately for both Sister Florence and me, she left, I think to retire, at the beginning of my grade five. She was replaced by a much younger nun called Sister Andrina. I thought she was young anyway, but then you could never tell with nuns. She had a mischievous sense of humour, and was a brilliant drop punt. She was the coach of our football side. Unfortunately we weren't all that good, but that had nothing to do with the quality of the coach. I suspect it was more due to do with the fact that Aussie Rules was not all that well known in Belgrade or Venice or wherever else the bulk of the kids at Our Lady of the Pines came from. Sister Andrina taught me and the rest of the students a love of the English language, and a

Sister Andrina.

voracious appetite for reading, no small feat when at least ninety per cent of the school had English as a second language.

Poetry had always left me cold, as it probably did most primary school kids, until Sister Andrina showed it to us in a completely different light. She was a big fan of Banjo Paterson, and of course Banjo Paterson was ideal for kids new to the country, simply because of his simplicity and the intense and evocative Australianness of his work. We listened agog to 'The Man from Snowy River' and 'Clancy of the Overflow', and laughed at the sheer cheekiness of 'The Geebung Polo Club' and 'The Man from Ironbark'. Each poem was a marvellous story, and to a kid as impressionable as me, there was nothing quite as thrilling as 'Murder, bloody murder, cried the man from Ironbark' after the barber drew the blunt edge of a hot razor across his throat. The humour was basic, and the imagery so darned clear. Sister Andrina made Paterson even more accessible by giving us geography and history lessons about the parts of Australia where the various poems were set.

Having thus captured the imagination of her young audience, Sister Andrina led us all into trickier territory, always with a solid background of information to keep us interested in what the poet was saying. And interested we were in the 'Dirty British coaster with a salt caked smoke stack butting through the channel in the mad March days' juxtaposed with 'Quinquireme of Nineveh from distant Ophir rowing home to haven in sunny Palestine' in John Masefield's 'Cargoes'. In the days before video, Sister Andrina's descriptions were played out before us as well as any David Lean epic.

To this day my favourite poem is Hilaire Belloc's 'Tarantella'. Sister Andrina explained that a tarantella was a particularly energetic and colourful dance that young Spanish maidens would perform, their bright multilayered dresses whirling around them as the spun. Then 'Stomp Stomp' went Sister Andrina's heavy black nun's shoes as she leapt onto the raised podium at the front of our classroom. The slow rhythmic clicking of her fingers as she slowly twirled and swirled in her drab, brown habit, gradually gained speed as 'The girl went chancing, glancing, dancing, backing and advancing,' in the flea-ridden tavern in the high Pyrenees where the wine 'tasted of the tar'. I was transfixed. No flamenco dancer was ever so young or beautiful or talented as Sister Andrina when she taught a motley bunch of kids from all over the world to love the 'Tarantella'.

* * * *

The end of year concerts at Our Lady of the Pines were something else again. The nuns could let all their creative energy run riot, with

In 1961 we moved out of the church and into a new two-room school.
The Bishop came down from Adelaide to bless the building.

willing participation from seven classes of would-be thespians just itching to tread the boards — well, at least that was true in my case. After months of rehearsal and preparation the school would stage a full-on, all singing, all dancing extravaganza. It's just a shame Hollywood didn't send a scout out to sign us up. I'm sure the various parts among the several 'acts' were judiciously bestowed by the two nuns, but the more theatrical amongst us would vie like mad to see how many acts we could get into. A lead role in 'Come to the Fair', a support role in 'Sing to Me Gypsy', plus special effects coordinator (flashing a torch on and off under red cellophane in the campfire scene) made up my year of triumph. Mama Cameron came to the concert that year and loved it, impressed that 'two women could do so much with so little'. I think the comment might have included the talent of certain budding performers.

The Nangwarry nuns lived not far from the school in a rented government house which they called the Convent. It was the typical fibro mill cottage that everyone in town lived in, distinguished by a wooden cross at the apex of the front gable. I always thought the place was a bit mysterious, with its dark interior and highly polished floorboards. It smelled of kerosene and Wundawax. I'm not sure how they got by, because they relied on hand-outs basically, and a lot of the families whose kids attended Our Lady of the Pines didn't have two bob to rub together. Thursday was 'fees' day, when all the kids would take along two shillings, but if they didn't have it no fuss was made.

Judging from the sparse nature of their furnishings, I think the nuns only just managed. Mum often provided an evening meal for them. I suppose when you were cooking for a tribe the size of ours, what are another two mouths to feed? After she'd prepared whatever we were having, she'd serve up two extra plates and wrap them in foil and tea towels to drop around to the Convent. Dessert 'wouldn't be necessary' Sister Florence told Mum. The moment she left, the new Principal, Sister Anthony, asked if 'it wouldn't be too much trouble' to reinstate the desserts.

Sometimes the nuns would visit our house on weekends or

during the holidays. Because of some silly rules at the time, the Sisters could never eat with us, but would have their lunch or dinner in a different room. I was amazed that they liked a shandy — I thought only parents drank that.

* * * *

At Our Lady of the Pines, I encountered a kid who was to become my nemesis for the next few years. His name was David Yeates and his family had a farm not far from Nangwarry. He was really good at sport, quite possibly because his build strongly resembled that of a whippet or a kangaroo dog. In fact his nickname was Roo, short for kangaroo dog. I on the other hand was built more like a beagle, and in the ironically cruel way that kids have, I was nicknamed Champ, because I was invariably last at any pursuit which required anything remotely approaching physical exertion. I pretty much got used to the teasing from most of the kids, it was fairly good natured. But Roo Yeates was somehow different, he always seemed to be able to wind me up beautifully, and was pretty quick with his fists if I dared respond in kind.

I came in for quite a number of hammerings, but on some very rare occasions I managed to dream up a delicious revenge. I soon learned that to be fleet of cunning could be many times more satisfying than being fleet of foot. Roo was the kind of kid who would help himself to any treat you might take to school, whatever it was, so generally you would keep it well concealed. This was the background for a particularly sweet revenge I devised with a packet of PK chewing gum on one memorable occasion. Carefully opening the packet, I placed each little gum 'pillow' on the low wall between the lavatories and the wash troughs. Then in front of an admiring audience I proceeded to pee all over them. After a short drying off time, I packed the chewies back into their wrapper and took them into the classroom. Here, of course, I made great play of taking the packet out of my pocket so that everyone could admire it. Roo rose to the bait beautifully, as I knew he would. With a quick swipe he snatched the chewies, sneering, 'I'll have those.' I tried to put on my most 'pissed off' face, but inside I was bursting to laugh. The kids who were in the know, perhaps being a little more farsighted than me, looked on with expressions ranging from nausea to ashen-faced terror.

The rock upon which I frequently perished when exacting revenge was the desire for others to share my triumph. After all, what's the use of doing something really dastardly if you're the only one who knows about it? I couldn't wait for the afternoon recess bell to ring. When it eventually did, we all trooped out into the playground, with a very interested group of onlookers watching with morbid fascination as Roo opened my packet of PK and made a great show of stuffing them all into his mouth at once. Kids, including me, fell about laughing and guffawing, while Roo began to smell a rat. Of course some tattletale had to spill the beans on me, and I returned to the classroom at the end of recess having been bashed to within an inch of my life. But boy, was it worth it.

Peeing competitions were very popular among the boys of Our Lady of the Pines. In the dank old cement urinal of the lavatory, we'd see who could pee furthest up the wall. It's amazing how much water a young bladder can hold in a desperate bid to build up pressure for such vital competition. Some of the heights reached, including those reached by myself, were truly impressive. If every lad who attended Our Lady of the Pines in the 1960s should suffer simultaneous prostate collapses in the not too distant future, I wouldn't be the least bit surprised.

* * * *

In 1961 bodgies and widgies became world famous. Movie magazines were full of *West Side Story,* and there were pictures of the Sharks and the Jets: to me they looked just like the bodgies and widgies we used to see at the pictures, or loitering around the milk bars in the Mount. Although it was a long time before *West Side Story* opened in Australia, I just knew it couldn't be too accurate, because I couldn't imagine the bodgies and widgies I was familiar with bursting into song every few minutes. Still, it scored big time at the Academy Awards that year, so someone must have thought it was all right. *Psycho* was also popular at about that time, and we were all busting to see it, but of course we weren't allowed to. Mum said it was far too scary for kids, and from what I could tell by the way grown-ups talked about it, it was far too scary for them too. All I knew was that something really spooky happened in the shower. I was glad we had a bath.

* * * *

On Mum's birthday, when I was ten and in my final year at Our Lady of the Pines, I had saved part of my lunch money each day for a week for a present for her. Add to that some money I'd conned off my brothers, and I ended up with about three bob. There was only one lunch shop in Nangwarry, and it was run by a foreign woman with long honey-coloured hair. When I say 'foreign', I think she was from England, but as ninety-nine point nine per cent of the town were 'new Australians', they were all piled into the 'dago' basket. I don't think we differentiated between nationalities. If you were a 'new Australian', you were a 'dago'. I told the honey-coloured hair woman it was my mum's birthday, and I wanted to buy a cake. She asked me how much I had, and I held out my handful of silver and copper coins. She paused a moment, took the money and said, 'That'll be okay, come back after school and the cake'll be ready for you.' I couldn't wait to get back to the shop after school broke up for the day. The lady with the honey coloured hair handed over the most beautiful cake I'd ever seen. It had candles on the top, and frilled paper around the sides. The paper was bright green and red and had the words 'Happy Birthday' written right around it.

The trip home was interminable, I was so careful not to trip, because to ruin such a magnificent creation would have been totally unforgivable. I walked along the pine break, sitting down every hundred yards or so because my arms were aching with the weight of it. The roar of the wind in the pines was like music to me, I was so excited. When I finally got home with it in one piece, I went inside to find my mum, pleased as punch with myself. Mum was peeling spuds at the sink. I held the cake out to her and said 'Happy Birthday.' She didn't say a word; she wiped her hands on her apron, took the cake from me and put it on the kitchen table. Then she sat down at the table, staring at the cake and bawled her eyes out.

5

The Stork and Stuff

For years we'd been told the 'stork' story whenever questions came up about where babies came from, and in our house that was fairly often. Things got a bit complicated though, when other kids at school reported stories involving rabbits and cabbage patches, but because Mum had told us that babies were delivered by storks, that had to be right.

Then one day Angelo Morandin came to school with the most bizarre story about where babies came from, I couldn't believe my ears. I was agog that a kid could dream up such a wild and wacky story. When I got home that day, with my eyes still popping out of my head, I told Mum what Angelo Morandin had told me, or I should say I *attempted* to tell Mum what Angelo Morandin had told me, because I'd only just started to relate the tale, chapter and verse, when Mum cut me right off. 'Don't you ever listen to that awful boy again,' she said. 'Do you think that humans are just like animals?' I have to say I was very happy to go back to the stork story. I thought it sounded an awful lot better than what Angelo

Morandin had told me. It was quite some time later before I realised that Angelo had told me the truth, the whole truth and nothing but the truth.

* * * *

My mum was always pregnant, not surprising when you think about how little she knew about the birds and bees. With all the kids already on the scene, she desperately needed some help around the house. Being miles out of Mount Gambier where most of the extended family were, it was a bit much to expect them to help out, so a lady from Nangwarry filled the bill.

Mrs Gonella was a big Italian woman with brown hair and kind eyes. She was the wife of Walter Gonella, who worked in Dad's mill. When she started with us she didn't speak any English, but despite that, she managed to communicate very well, mainly by using her hands a lot. Mrs Gonella helped Mum with cleaning the house and she also did some cooking. She made basic authentic Italian food, which we always looked forward to. She had a pasta 'machina' as she called it. To make pasta, she'd start with a huge mountain of flour on the laminex kitchen table, then hollow out a crater in the centre of it. Into this crater she'd crack a dozen eggs and some salt, and then gradually fold in the sides with her hands until she had a huge ball of pasta dough. Then she would break manageable lumps off the dough ball and feed them through the rollers of her machina. Out the other end would emerge long flat strips, the rollers serving much like a miniature wringer on an old-fashioned washing machine. The flat strips were then fed through a cutter on the same machine to form the spaghetti strands.

If there was no meat in the fridge for the pasta sauce, there was plenty walking around the yard. To catch one of our free range chooks was not an easy feat, yet Mrs Gonella made it look like the simplest task on earth. She'd scatter a handful of wheat and while the chooks were busy, head down, pecking away, she'd move with a swiftness that was impressive for a substantial woman. Grabbing a chook by its legs, she'd quickly stand on its head with one foot and yank its legs suddenly, breaking its neck and killing it instantly. It was totally humane, but a bit of a shock to the system when you weren't expecting to see it ... Mum almost passed out! Then began the fascinating bit. Mrs Gonella would gut the chook, carefully sorting around in the giblets for all the tasty bits. She wasted nothing, and would end up with a little pile of heart, liver, gizzard and so on, which she'd rinse off and then chop finely to go into the most delicious pasta sauce you've ever tasted, not least because she used to bottle all her own tomato sauce when tomatoes were plentiful in the summer. She'd store literally hundreds of old beer bottles full of the delicious pulp, to last through the year. About this time I decided Australia needed more migrants, especially Italians.

The Gonellas had kids of their own, Anna and Maria, who were born in Italy, and another daughter and twin boys born in Australia. On Fridays, when Mum drove in to Mount Gambier to do the family shopping, we kids would often go to the Gonellas' after school. Their house was pretty much like all the other houses in Nangwarry, very sparsely furnished. Some of the furniture I recognised as old stuff of ours that Mum and Dad had given them to help set up. The house always smelled terrific, with the large friendly presence of Mrs Gonella looking after whatever it was she had simmering away on the old Metters stove. As soon as we arrived we'd have lovely crusty Italian bread with cheese, or sweet homemade biscuits twisted into the shape of little bows. There'd also be the smell of coffee percolating, though despite its lovely aroma, I thought it looked and tasted like mud.

The Gonellas and their friends used to make their own wine. They bought the grapes just up the road a bit at Coonawarra, in the days before Coonawarra was as famous as it is now, so the wine should have been all right. However after they did whatever it was they did to the grapes, they ended up with the most disgusting tasting paint stripper imaginable. Mr Gonella, however, thought it was very good, and when we visited after school we'd have a glass, heavily diluted with water, because that was what Italian kids did. It still tasted shocking, but we felt terribly grown up. I can still see my mum's face, arriving to pick us up one Friday evening to be greeted with the sight of her darlings elegantly sipping homemade plonk out of Vegemite glasses. Mrs Gonella got an ear bashing, but she held her own and insisted it was the right way to teach children the joys of wine — and on this, I was on her side!

* * * *

The Brown Joeys at Our Lady of the Pines taught us a lot about politics, at least from their perspective. They'd have us completely agog with stories of what would happen should the Communists ever take over Australia. They showed us terrible pictures of mounted soldiers with swords dripping blood running down terrified women and children. They didn't point out that the pictures actually depicted the Czar's soldiers cutting down the peasants at the time of the revolution, but that was beside the point. It was Russia wasn't it? And if it happened in Russia it had to be bad. Over the years I spent countless hours on my knees praying to the Blessed Virgin for 'the conversion of Russia', for unless that happened — we were told — we were all surely doomed.

Among the horror stories they told us about the Communist way of life was how Russian children couldn't live with their parents during the day. They were all flung into day care centres while both of their poor parents had to go to work. This was undoubtedly the worst thing I had ever heard of. Just imagine not having a mum waiting for you when you got home! Even Mrs Gonella, who worked at our place, was home in time for her kids when they got out of school. As far as I knew, everyone's mum was at home.

The Devil was big in the sixties too, even bigger than the Russians, and that's saying something. The Devil could get you for all sorts of things and was watching your every move for the tiniest slip-up so that he could move right on in. Some of the things he could get you for seemed pretty minor to me, but you could never be too careful. 'An idle mind is the Devil's playground,' they told us. No problem for me on that account, I thought, my imagination was too active for the Devil to get much of a look in there. We also knew that 'Idle hands do the Devil's work,' which proved a bit trickier, because it was sometimes difficult to decide what was just plain mischief and what was the 'Devil's work'. Little wonder that

'The Devil made me do it,' was an excuse often bandied about.

Pupil free days and teachers' in-house training days were unheard of in the sixties, at least at the schools I went to. The only break from the daily grind of schoolwork came when someone important visited the school and a 'half-day off' was declared. A visit from a State Governor was particularly welcome since they never stayed too long (probably because they had a dozen other schools to visit), their speeches were short, there was plenty of pomp and flag waving, and they always had very regal looking large black cars, with a driver wearing a cap. The Archbishop could be relied on for the occasional 'half-dayer', although the pleasure was sometimes dimmed by a sung Mass which would go on interminably.

The best visit of all was from local girl Tricia Reschke who was crowned Miss Australia in 1962. Tania Verstak had won the year before, which was a bit puzzling, since she came from Russia and anything Russian just had to be plain bad. However, as always, the nuns came to the rescue and explained that Tania was a 'white' Russian rather than a 'red' Russian, whose family had come to Australia to escape the clutches of the Communists — so that made it all right. I'd thought Tania Verstak was the most beautiful girl I'd ever seen, but then I'd only ever seen her in magazines. Tricia Reschke I actually got to see in the flesh, and suddenly she was the most beautiful. Bear in mind that these sweeping thoughts belonged to the time in my life before I ever laid eyes on Dusty Springfield.

* * * *

Although my family was far from wealthy, we were much better off than most of the families in Nangwarry, many of them migrants and refugees from the war who were just starting to rebuild their lives. Another family who were better off than most and lived a little out of town — like us — were the Gardiners, who ran Nangwarry Station. Stan and Molly Gardiner had three kids, Julian, Ian and Phillipa, who were roughly the same age as Peter, Charles and myself. They also had a beige International van, which their kids thought was pretty hot since it was the largest automobile in town.

Nangwarry Station was east of Nangwarry towards the Victorian Border. We had plenty of great times there, including working bees to raise funds for the church and school. How this worked was that men from the parish would volunteer to do labouring jobs like digging post holes when the station had a large project like fencing to be done. The wages that would otherwise have been due to the men would be paid into the school fund. People would take picnic lunches and barbecues, and while the men worked, the ladies would provide sandwiches and billy tea while the kids just mucked around. In this way, and with heaps of other fundraising fetes and cake stalls etcetera, sufficient money was raised to start work on two new classrooms.

Nangwarry Station was occasionally the venue for a big Picnic Fete, organised by a committee from the school with Mrs Gardiner overseeing it all. Hundreds of townies would turn up for the horse and buggy rides, shearing exhibitions and sheepdogs showing off. There'd be a huge barbecue and a barn dance in the woolshed at the end of the day for those who weren't too exhausted to stand up. If

*On the verandah at Nangawarry Station. Me in the foreground then,
clockwise from left, my brother Malcolm, Ian and Julian Gardiner and
my brothers Charles and Peter.*

we kids behaved ourselves and the babies weren't making too much
fuss, we could stay for the first little while of the barn dance. The
band — piano, drums and saxophone — played the standard
oldies, though sometimes they'd have a go at some of the more
recent 'hits' and the younger adults would jive and rock and roll.
The oldies didn't consider that to be dancing at all.

The Nangwarry Station homestead was a beautiful old building
which had grown like Topsy over the years, with verandahs closed
in, etcetera. It had massively thick stone walls, making it deliciously

cool in summer, and it seemed as if every room in the house had a fireplace, which made it cosy in winter. The Gardiners had a housekeeper called Mrs Bradley and I sometimes overheard the grown-ups murmuring about Mrs Bradley 'liking a drink'. We thought she was terrific, she always had jugs of cordial and milk in the cool room.

Stan Gardiner was my patron for my confirmation, when I took the extra name Gerard, after Saint Gerard Majella. So now I had the splendid moniker Eoin Harrap Gerard Cameron. Gerard was also the name of our newest baby, born in the Penola hospital, a beautiful blonde haired baby with goitrous blue eyes and I adored him. Stan Gardiner was a man of few words, but a kind man. When I went out to stay at the station I used to go around the stock with him in the horse and gig. On cold winter mornings the air would be full of the steam of our exhalations, and the horse's, the smell of grass, the rain, the wet leather and the horse's farts.

* * * *

Roo Yeates' grandparents lived on a farm the other side of Dad's mill, about three-quarters of a mile from our house. They were very old. They kept a kookaburra in a wired-in area under a tank stand, and fed it raw meat. The kookaburra would proceed to 'kill' the meat by picking it up in its beak and thrashing it on the ground, the way they would kill mice and small reptiles in the wild. Occasionally we might see a kookaburra flying along with great difficulty, a small dead snake hanging from its beak. The story goes that to kill a snake, the kookaburra would take it to a great height and then drop it. I couldn't understand how it was the snake didn't just bite the kookaburra and kill it first.

Granny Yeates had a big old fridge filled with small bottles of Coca Cola. In those days Coke from the small bottles tasted so good, especially when it was so cold it 'burned' your throat.

Old Mr and Mrs Yeates had a bloke called Mick, who lived in a room at the back of their house. I'm not sure if he was a relative they didn't want anyone to know about or whether he was a former farm worker they'd kept on after he retired. I think he did a few odd jobs around the place but that was it. He seemed to me to spend most of his time enjoying a drink or three.

Mick had an Austin ute, dark green. Come to think of it, I don't think I ever saw an Austin ute of any other colour. One day during a school holiday break I was wandering up the road when Mick pulled over and asked me if I wanted a lift. I think he forgot to drop me off at our gate, and took me into a little town called Kalangadoo, about seven miles away, where he stopped at a pub. He gave me ten bob to occupy myself with and went in to have a few quiet beers. Ten bob was an enormous amount of money, and I bought more lollies than I could jump over. Meanwhile it was nearing dark and the alert had gone out at home that I had 'disappeared'. Just before sunset we were discovered in a drainage ditch, having run off the road on the way home. Mick was sound asleep behind the wheel having wet his pants, and I was crook as a dog from overdosing on lollies. Once again I got the familiar lecture about not getting into cars with strangers, Mum and Dad conveniently overlooking the fact that Mick was hardly a stranger.

* * * *

In the early sixties, most Australians didn't eat a lot of chicken, except at Christmas and Easter, even though just about everyone we knew kept chooks. Even people who lived in town invariably had a chookyard at the bottom of the garden. We had plenty of room at Nangwarry, and Dad built really huge chookyards behind a big machinery shed. He bought hundreds of chicks which he kept in small pens with incubator lights. He also had some ducks, but I think they were a bit trickier to rear. At one time Mum was keeping some duck eggs warm at the bottom of our slow combustion stove. We had heard that chicks bond with the first thing they see when they're hatched, and in the case of the ducklings this was my mum. They would follow her around the kitchen, chirping away, which was all very cute. Unfortunately they also shat all over the place, so they were soon banished to their own little pen in the shed, with a light bulb for warmth. I'm not sure that Dad's chook breeding was a runaway success, because the foxes from the surrounding forests regularly had a field day. They were brilliant at devising ways of getting into the supposedly fox-proof yards, and on the painful one or two occasions when someone accidentally left the chookyard gate open at night, it was smorgasbord for Brer Fox and his mates.

Just alongside the chook runs was a huge machinery shed, which the guy who owned the property before us had used as a workshop. He was a carpenter or cabinet-maker of some kind I think: there were lots of workbenches and plenty of power points. A lot of heavy power tools had obviously been used in the shed, and it was wired for three phase electricity, which was almost the downfall of my older brother Peter. He had already started college in the Mount, and was learning about physics and stuff we'd never heard of. One day he was giving us a little lesson in the mode of Professor Julius Sumner Miller on the electrical conductivity of certain materials. I'm not clear as to the exact nature of Peter's experiment, but it sure impressed us — and Mum, who saw the brilliant blue flash from the house next door. Peter was thrown from the bench where he was experimenting, and there was a smell in the air like singed duck. His hair had gone a bit frizzy and was burned at the ends, and he was shaking violently. Oddly, he seemed to lose interest in physics experiments after that. We were also permanently banned from going anywhere near the workbenches in the shed, and brainwashed about how close Peter had come to no longer being with us.

* * * *

Every kid should have a good mate, and though we had left the Mount, mine was still my cousin Robin. He was the only kid I knew who could match me when it came to dreaming up adventurous schemes. In some areas he actually outdid me — pyrotechnics, for one. Cracker night was a very big deal, something we looked forward to with great anticipation in the lead up to the fifth of November. Like so many fun things, Guy Fawkes Night was eventually discouraged, and finally banned, but not before we had many years of excellent if dangerous times. Each year, kids would be badly burned, have bits of fingers blown off, or suffer various other injuries as a result of cracker night.

If you had the resources, you could stockpile a bonfire for days. If you had a grown-up to help, you could really do a professional job, and this wasn't difficult to arrange because most dads liked cracker night as much as we did, if not more. If you really wanted to go the whole hog, you could make a Guy Fawkes, a stuffed scarecrow to burn at the stake in the middle of the bonfire. If you had the willpower and a degree of self-discipline, you could store up a very handy little arsenal in readiness for the big night. When you added Robin's ordnance to what we had collected, many a small military power might have been green with envy.

The girls had fireworks of their own, which they'd squeal and carry on about — sparklers, Catherine Wheels and Mount Vesuvius Volcanoes. As far as crackers went, they were okay I suppose, but mainly for looks only. They fizzed and spluttered, and threw out showers of sparks and pretty colours. What we were into was the big bang, and the bigger the bang the better. Tom Thumbs had their place, usually a handful lit at once and thrown among the girls just to watch them scatter. They weren't particularly frightening — they just made 'phht phht' sounds as they went off in rapid succession — but they scared the hell out of the girls. Then we got to the ha'penny bungers, which could be held in the fingers if you were seriously brave. Next the penny bunger, not to be held under any circumstances. The three-penny bunger could blow a spud out of a pipe over quite a considerable distance, and the granddaddy of them all, the eight-penny bunger, could make a letterbox and surrounding shrubbery disappear. It could also get one into very serious bother. The eight-penny bunger looked like the sticks of dynamite you saw in cowboy pictures when they were blowing up train tracks. Skyrockets were high on our list too; the only trouble with them was we never got to set them off because the dads wanted the fun of doing it themselves. They'd stick the tail into a tall brown beer bottle then light the taper and stand back. If a few bob had been spent on the rocket, it was probably capable of going into low earth orbit before exploding and scaring the living daylights out of every dog within cooee. Our dogs would spend a few days each year around Guy Fawkes night rolling their eyes and hyperventilating.

Robin had a genius for such things, and he developed all manner of sophisticated weaponry — we'd come a long way from the old bow and arrow. Out of a piece of metal water pipe, he fashioned a marble gun. One end of the pipe was sealed, and the idea was to light a ha'penny bunger and drop it down the pipe, followed by a marble. You then very quickly took aim at your target. The results were impressive: you could shoot a hole through a sheet of corrugated iron. How no one was killed or maimed is yet another of life's miracles. It was Robin too who discovered the explosive qualities of asbestos thrown into a very hot open fire. On days when Dad burned up piles of accumulated rubbish, we'd wait till the bonfire had died down to glowing coals, then break a sheet of asbestos into chunks about a foot square. After we'd thrown them on the coals, we'd hit the deck and wait for the explosion. Sometimes they'd go off almost immediately, other times it'd take a minute or so, but it was always worth the wait.

Our house at Nangwarry had a wide verandah across about a half of its frontage. The cement on top of the verandah had expansion grooves running in straight lines from the house outwards, so that the grooves pointed out towards the main road. In a burst of sheer brilliance, Robin came up with a use for the otherwise hopeless sixpenny rockets. As far as we were concerned they were useless — they didn't fly very high, and didn't go bang at the end — I suppose you couldn't expect much more for sixpence. Robin discovered that the expansion grooves on the verandah made a wonderful guided launcher for the rockets. Who else would have thought of firing them horizontally rather than vertically? Now they became very interesting.

The sixpenny rockets were about eight inches long, very narrow, and with paper fins on the tail. With a little experimentation, we found that you could manipulate the tail fins until they were shaped more like the tail of a conventional aircraft. This way, the rocket could be fired from the verandah grooves and shoot across the front lawn towards the highway at approximately two feet above ground level. Across the highway was a wide ploughed pine-break, where the spent rocket could fall harmlessly to the ground — although this was not our plan.

With a stopwatch, we calculated how long the rocket took to reach the highway from the launch pad, and also how long the taper fuse took to ignite the rocket. We thus engineered what was to be the ultimate success for us rocket scientists, a direct hit on an unsuspecting car or truck. We set up an elaborate phone system, using a length of string stretched tight between two Aktavite tins. Aktavite tins were very easy to come by at our place, because it was supposedly good for helping lactation, and lactating was something Mum was doing an awful lot of in those days. With our phone system, one of us would hide in the scrub on the block next door while the other would be on alert, match poised ready to strike at the signal that a potential target had reached a certain point on the highway.

We were in the most part singularly unsuccessful. We probably fired more rockets than Woomera without anything even approaching a strike. I imagine some motorists might have been slightly surprised at something whizzing past their windscreen, or perhaps catching the merest glimpse of a flash in their rearview mirror. As with most things in life, persistence pays off, and thus the big day came. I was the forward scout, hanging out in the wattle trees next door. Robin, the chief rocket scientist, was desperate for success. The target on this occasion turned out to be a motorcycle. We'd never even attempted to have a go at one of them before, considering them far too small to have a chance of a strike. 'Ignite rocket,' I said into the Aktavite tin.

'Roger wilco,' Robin replied. We had no idea what that meant, but Biggles said it all the time into his two-way in the radio serials, so we knew it must be important. As the motorbike drew almost level with the house, the rocket was away with a loud hiss, and a trail of flame and smoke streaking away from the front verandah. Bullseye! A direct hit! We could not believe it — and neither could the motorbike rider. To say he was amazed would be an under-statement. The rocket had lodged in the cooling fins on the motorbike's motor, still spurting flame and smoke as it spent itself. The rider was struggling to control his bike as he wobbled off the road and went over sideways, bouncing and scraping through the gravel and into the bush.

Robin and I knew immediately that this time we'd gone too far. I don't think we imagined for a moment our 'rocket' would actually hit anything, but it had, and suddenly all our chooks had come home to roost. Amazingly, the motorbike rider wasn't even slightly injured, just incredibly shaken. Mind you not nearly as shaken as us two rocket scientists when he knocked on the door of our house and told Dad what had happened. Luckily for us, his bike was okay; he was just very upset, or things could have been far worse for Robin and me. But the holiday was ruined. After Dad found us skulking in the bush between our house and the mill, Robin was sent back to the Mount, I was belted and a brilliant future in ballistics was nipped in the bud.

6

Kangaroo Club and Television

Although television came to Australia in time for the 1956 Melbourne Olympics, it was unheard of in our part of the world. We knew the Americans had it, but imagined it was so far into the future for us it wasn't worth bothering about. What you never had you never missed, and as far as entertainment went, who could ask for more than the radio? After school we made sure we were home in time for the serials. I was a member of the Kangaroo Club, which meant that I got my birthday announced on the radio, which was a darned good thing, because being born on the fourth of January, so close to Christmas and in the middle of the holidays, the date could easily be forgotten, and *has* been. Anyway, as a member of the Kangaroo Club, your birthday was announced to the world so everyone would know, and a magic flying horse called Gandy would deliver a Freddo Frog to a secret location around your house or garden. Gandy didn't speak, but each afternoon he'd clip clop in to the studios of 5SE, the Mount Gambier station of the Advertiser Broadcasting Network based in Adelaide. After a couple of whinnies, Gandy would pass on to the announcer the messages he had for the birthday kids, then clip clop again out of the studio. You could hear his hooves pounding off into the distance as he took off to deliver the chocolate frogs, his speed was quite astounding. One of the great joys in life was to hear the announcer say, 'Happy Birthday to Eoin Cameron of Nangwarry from Mum and Dad and all the family. Gandy has put your Freddo Frog behind the water softener.'

The serial I loved most on the afternoon kids' show was *Biggles, the Adventures of Commander Bigglesworth*, by Captain W. E. Johns. It was just amazing, the number of scrapes Biggles could get out of, 'bloodied but unbowed', despite the best efforts of every evil dude ever dreamed up. He even saved the earth from aliens in 'Biggles and the case of the Blue Ray'. What a man! Biggles would always come through, although you invariably had to wait for the next episode to see how he was going to make it from his latest 'scrape'. The ABC had kids' stuff too, shows like *The Argonauts*, but I thought the way they ran their club with members taking on daggy names like 'Julius' and 'Paris' was too sappy by half.

At night time there were serials for grown-ups — inevitably boring, and a signal that it was time for bed, but Mum and Dad would be transfixed by shows like *No Holiday for Halliday*, *Campbell's Kingdom* and *The Wake of the Red Witch*. We were also forced to listen to the Catholic Hour on occasions, now that was *truly* excruciating. There was an American guy called Bishop Fulton Sheen who was something of a media star at the time. His sermons were probably okay, but not for kids our age. We'd end up with the rosary after the broadcast, because as the bishop would always say as he finished each broadcast, 'The family that prays together stays together.'

Most of our radio listening was now done sitting around a cream console model which was kept on the kitchen bench. We could stuff down Vegemite or peanut butter sandwiches or jam scones while listening breathlessly to Biggles. In the lounge room, the grown-ups had the Philips stereogram, which was the very height of sophistication and the envy of all who saw and heard it. Words could not describe how cool the Philips was. The dark polished wooden cabinet was roughly the size and shape of a twin-tub washing machine. When you slid the top back, a transformation would take place. As the top disappeared into the back of the cabinet, the front opened downwards to form a shelf and there, ensconced in polished blonde wood, was the radio tuner and felt-covered turntable, with a stylus arm which could be switched to 'regular' or 'micro-groove', depending on the record. This was the machine the word 'snazzy' was invented for. Below the fold-down front shelf was a huge fabric-covered speaker behind a wooden lattice, and on either side of that, cupboards which opened out to house your record collection.

Mum and Dad had some pop singles of the day, and some old seventy-eights they'd been given. The seventy-eights were mainly yodelling cowboy stuff which left us pretty cold, but they did have Marty Robbins' 'A White Sport Coat' and Clarence 'Frogman' Henry's 'But I Do'. There was a micro-groove album which I think might have come with the radiogram, 'Ken Griffin and His Organ'; it was mainly older melodic stuff, and Mum and Dad used to dance to that a lot.

There was a story doing the rounds that snakes could be charmed by music, and we proved it one day with the Philips stereogram and Ken Griffin and his organ. Someone spotted a large snake on the front verandah, just outside the lounge room doors. Dad was summoned, but before he arrived the snake slid down the gap at the back of the verandah and disappeared under the house. Mum reckoned it was worth trying the music trick to get the snake to come out again. The Philips was shifted to stand directly over that part of the lounge room floor under which the snake had disappeared. Ken Griffin was put on and turned up loud. Minutes later, we watched in horrified fascination from the safety of the lounge room, as the snake reappeared, swaying its head from side to side, seemingly entranced by the music. It didn't get to do too much swinging from side to side mind you, because one swing from Dad's spade put an end to all that. I'm not sure what exactly that proved about snakes and music. Mum reckoned it had more to do with the vibrations; because the Philips had such a huge speaker, the bass was quite earth-shaking.

* * * *

Mama Cameron was quite a bit younger than Mama Harrap, and still had a couple of her kids living with her, Allen and Jean. Aunty Jean was so close to our own ages she seemed more like a cousin to us, and it was she who told me the first dirty joke I ever heard. It went like this: one day there was a girl who had a dog called Titswobble. One day the dog went missing, and the girl searched everywhere for it, going up and down the street calling out,

'Titswobble, Titswobble.' She saw the milkman on his rounds, and ran up to him saying, 'Oh please milkman, have you seen my dog Titswobble?' — 'No I haven't,' replied the milkman. Next she saw the policeman directing traffic and ran up to him and said, 'Policeman, have you seen my dog Titswobble?' — 'No sorry dear,' said the policeman. In desperation the girl went to the boy next door. 'Have you seen my Titswobble?' she said. To which the boy replied, 'No, but I'd like to!' I thought it was the most clever, vulgar, funny story I'd ever heard. It earned me a few clips around the ear upon repeating it, but it was worth it.

My appetite for sophisticated humour was soon plumbing the very depths of early sixties vulgarity with the classic, 'Milk, milk, lemonade, round the corner chocolate's made!' We'd fall about in fits while those affronted would hightail it to dob on us.

Aunty Jean was terrific fun, although in retrospect she must have found visits to our house something of a ordeal. On one memorable weekend afternoon, a couple of my brothers and I lured her to an old quarry in the bush behind Dad's mill. This wasn't difficult, since the bush behind the mill was really interesting, with lots of old gravel pits which had filled with water to make miniature lakes. The bush was alive with rabbits, so there were plenty of things to keep kids occupied. Dad used some of the disused gravel quarries to dump sawdust from the mill. Overhanging one of the larger quarries was a big old red gum tree, its branches spreading out about thirty feet above the sawdust mound below. We had tied a rope to one of the sturdier branches, and used to perform Tarzan acts, pounding our chests and yodelling as we swung out over the abyss — or rather, the crocodile infested waters below.

No way was Jean prepared to have a go on the Tarzan swing, she was far too scared. But we thought she shouldn't miss such a treat, and so we tied her to the rope and swung her off the cliff anyway. This was the first time I had seen a person go truly hysterical. The most frightening part about it for us was not the state Aunty Jean was in, but the state we'd be in after Dad found out what we'd done. We tried to strike a deal with Jean as she hung there hyperventilating over the sawdust. In her fleeting moments of sanity, she would have promised anything, as long as we got her down. When, between sobs, she promised she wouldn't tell on us, we hauled her back to the cliff top, an emotional wreck. Of course, the moment she got her feet on the ground she sprinted home to report in loving detail, what her nephew 'savages' had done to her. Mama Cameron took Aunty Jean home in high dudgeon. We of course got thrashed! Jean must have forgiven us, because within weeks we were good mates again.

* * * *

Living next door to a timber mill provided all manner of opportunities for adventure and mayhem. At school we were constantly reminded about the importance of 'Guardian Angels', and having survived the mill, I am in no doubt whatsoever of the existence of such creatures.

As the pine logs were fed across the benches and into the saws, the resulting sawdust was sucked through a giant blower and deposited into hoppers which looked like little houses built up high on stilts. A truck would be positioned below one of these hoppers and the truck driver would haul on a lever which made the metal doors of the hopper slide back, so that a load of sawdust would drop into the truck. I'm not sure what weight of sawdust would make up a load, but it was certainly a lot.

When we knew a load of sawdust was due to be carted away to be dumped in the quarry, we'd stealthily climb into the hopper, sit on top of the sawdust, and then get dumped into the back of the truck when the driver opened the lever. Quite often one of us would get half buried, and have to be dug out by the others as the truck trundled along the bumpy bush track to the quarry. Upon reaching the quarry, the driver would back up to the cliff edge, then set the tipper going to empty the load. We'd hold on to the leading edge of the tipper tray, dangling out into space as the load of sawdust emptied. Eventually one of the drivers rumbled to what we were up to. After a good belting from Dad, and promises that we'd never do anything so stupid again in our lives, we changed strategy. Instead of hiding in the hopper, now we waited until the truck was loaded and beginning its slow trundle to the quarry. The track passed through copses of dense silver wattle trees, which formed a sort of natural tunnel. We would climb up into the wattles, wait for the lumbering old tipper, then drop silently onto the load of sawdust as it passed below.

The huge GMC six-cylinder two-stroke diesel motors which drove the sawbenches at the mill were originally fitted to Bren gun carriers and tanks during the Second World War. Dad and Uncle Allen picked them up as war surplus, along with the Blitz four- and six-wheel drive trucks which they converted to carry logs — ideal for the swampy conditions in the south-east. In the depths of winter, the sawbench motors would be very sluggish to start, so to keep the batteries from going flat, Dad kick-started them with ether. He would soak a cloth with a small amount of ether, and hold it over the engine's air intake as they cranked the starter motor over. Because of the dangers involved, not just with the motors, but no doubt the ether as well, the engine room was the most secure part of the mill. It was only open when the men were working there during the day, and was securely locked and bolted at night and over the weekend. All that security signified to our inquisitive minds that there must be something fascinating indeed in the engine room.

One weekend, we managed to get one of the engine room windows open, and thus we came upon the mysterious ether bottles, large brown demijohn affairs. We took the lid off one, and each of us had a cautious sniff — whhhhoooooooeeeeeeeeee! Unfortunately the ether also induced nausea and vomiting, although we soon turned that into another bit of fun for us. I don't know how many 'new Australian' kids from town we lured to the mill to take a peek at the 'magic' bottles. 'One sniff, and incredible things would happen,' we told them. Then we'd fall about holding our sides, struggling to see through tears of laughter, as a trail of disoriented kids staggered back along the pine breaks, doubling over occasionally to throw up. God only knows how they explained their state to their parents. One moment, perfectly healthy kids heading out to the Camerons' to play — home half an hour later, listless and puking all over the place.

* * * *

One day I came to some fairly serious grief myself while mucking around at the mill. Climbing over a pile of logs which were stacked ready for the benchmen to start on Monday morning, I slipped and fell onto the sawbench. Of course, being the weekend, it wasn't in operation; even so, the teeth of the circular saw were razor sharp, and I very neatly sliced the ball of my left foot through to the bone. The cut was so neat and so surgical I didn't even feel it straightaway. Then, climbing back onto the logs, I felt as though I had something stuck to the bottom of my foot. I kept trying to kick it off until, when I looked down at it, I truly freaked. What I was trying to kick off was half the sole of my left foot. It was hanging down, a great bloody, sawdust-encrusted flap of meat. Mum almost passed out when she saw it, and after about five minutes the pain had really set in, so I was almost passing out too. Doctor, stitches, more unpleasantness all round — this was getting to be a bit of a routine.

Dad really couldn't talk about my carelessness too much; he has no tops on any of his fingers. One memorable afternoon at Nangwarry he had been putting some firewood through a small bench saw when he came in to Mum, clutching his hand with blood going everywhere and a couple of fingers missing. We kids were dispatched to look for them and soon found them in the sawdust. We brought them back in a towel, relishing the gore, but Mum couldn't bear to look at them, she'd gone very green around the gills for some reason. Dad and the fingers were taken off to hospital where the doctors had a go at stitching them back on. Looking at Dad's hands, it's hard to say whether they were successful or not.

* * * *

We had the distinction of being the first household in the district to get a television set. The nearest stations were in Adelaide, about two hundred and fifty miles to the north-north-west, and Melbourne, a little closer than that to the east. We had to have a television 'tower' installed — it was much more than an aerial. Depending upon whether you were trying to pick up stations in Adelaide or Melbourne, the tower could be swung around to face in the general direction of the transmitters on Mount Lofty or those in the Dandenongs. Even with the tower, reception was shocking. Some nights, particularly in overcast conditions, we might get a few hours of 'perfect' television, but most of the time we'd sit staring at a snowstorm, the sound fading in and out. Once while trying to pick up the ABC from Adelaide, we got a perfect test pattern, not from ABS2, but from ABW2, the ABC in Perth. It only lasted half an hour or so, but we were wildly impressed. Dad tried everything to improve the picture. He bought a booster for the aerial, which scarcely made any difference, and we even covered the screen in blue cellophane — that was supposed to cut out the 'snow', but as far as I could see the only difference was we watched blue snow instead of white snow.

Our first TV set was a seventeen-inch Astor on fashionable spindly legs, but it wasn't very good, and after a few weeks Dad took it back and traded up to a twenty-one inch solid state Healing — now that was so cool it was positively frigid! It wasn't long before Channel Six began telecasting from Ballarat, which meant we got longer snatches of programs like *Seahunt*, *Ben Casey* and *77 Sunset*

Strip during the snowstorms. Angela Stacey was the female presenter on Channel Seven in Adelaide. I thought she was stunning, with her piles of bouffant hair in the style of Dusty Springfield (not that I had yet, at this stage, laid eyes on Dusty Springfield).

Kids would occasionally come to our place after school to catch *Flipper* and *Torchy the Battery Boy* or *Clutch Cargo* and his pals Spinner and Paddlefoot between 'snowstorms'. Mum would bring out some pretty impressive afternoon teas, like Kia-Ora cordial with rainbow cake. Mum would try anything new, and when White Wings started flogging multicoloured cake mixes, we had them. There were three packets in the box, and the idea was to mix the different colours separately, then swirl them together before baking. I used to dissect the cake to see if the brown (chocolate) part tasted any different from the white (vanilla) or pink (strawberry) parts. As far as I could tell, they all tasted the same.

* * * *

By the time I was in grade six we'd been living at Nangwarry for a couple of years, but we were often back in the Mount. Family functions, sporting events, working bees and school fetes were all good opportunities to get together with my cousins and old school friends. Mum's specialty for school fetes was homemade honeycomb. She'd make tons of it, and when it was cool, break it up into slabs and wrap it in clear cellophane. She *had* to make tons of it, because we 'sampled' as much honeycomb before we left home as was ever sold at a fete. Other mums made toffee apples and biscuits etcetera, and the dads had a hot dog stand, and ran the lucky dips and chocolate wheel. People would donate all sorts of stuff for the lucky dips. Presents were wrapped and placed in old tea chests covered in crepe paper.

At a fete run by the Mercy nuns at Port MacDonnell, there was a threepenny dip and a sixpenny dip, and of course you assumed the more lavish items would be in the more expensive dip. I wangled a bob out of Mama Harrap so I could have two goes at the sixpenny dip. My first surprise was a disappointment to say the least — a pink comb, brush and mirror in a shiny plastic bag — I was disgusted. My second dip made up for it though, it was *much* more interesting. It turned out that the dips had been put together by Sister Margaret, the same Sister Margaret who had taught me altar boy Latin! Sister Margaret had mellowed somewhat with age, although it seemed she'd also lost the plot a bit. My second dip was a plain green bottle, about the size and shape of a 'Texan' hair treatment bottle. 'Texan' was the stuff you combed through your hair when it was wet; it was non-greasy, but set so hard you could whack a kid on the head with a wooden ruler, and you'd stand more chance of splitting the ruler than the kid's head — all it made was a 'clunk' sound. 'Texan' could transform a perfectly normal head into tortoiseshell in ten minutes. Anyway, out of the dip came this plain green bottle which looked like 'Texan', but wasn't! I was bitterly disappointed until I took the lid off and took a whiff — it was unbelievable!

I'd never experienced anything quite so awful. Mama Harrap identified the mysterious substance as smelling salts, and tried to take the bottle off me — no way! I had one of the best days of my life. Every kid in Port MacDonnell was wandering around with their eyes out on stalks, sneezing and hyperventilating. It sure made up for the girls' beauty set. One thing about smelling salts which always puzzled me though, was that they were supposed to bring people around who had passed out. You could also make perfectly conscious people pass out, as Robin and I proved with his sister Cheryl when we held her down and made her sniff the bottle.

* * * *

Around this time, when I was about ten, I had my first trip to Adelaide. I was almost sick with excitement. We drove in through the Adelaide hills at sunset, and the lights of the city spread out below were like something out of a fairy tale. I thought it was the most beautiful sight I'd ever seen.

My Aunty Thelma lived in Adelaide. She was what my mother would have described as 'a bit common' had she not been my mum's sister. She was however very kind-hearted and would let us kids (and her own, our cousins) get away with anything. I think her kids were pretty close to being bodgies and widgies, if not in fact the real thing. Jimmy was about five years older than me, so he must have been around fifteen, and Millie was about seventeen. Jimmy was fat and wore the required tight jeans that had the leather patch with his name burnt into it, and Millie wore stretchy black slacks and fluorescent tops. She also had lots of hair and heaps of make-up, and they both smoked like trains.

We went to John Martins store in the city where you could buy a snowball from a vending machine — you put in threepence and out came a chocolate coated marshmallow ball, rolled in coconut. I marvelled at the wonders of modern science, and wondered whether a man in the machine was poking the snowballs through the opening every time someone put threepence in. I thought that might be a job you'd get tired of very quickly, especially after you'd eaten your fill of snowballs. A far more exciting job, I thought, was that of the lift man. They looked great in their smart suits and caps, and their memories were truly amazing — they knew everything there was on every floor, and could recite the list of most of the stuff before the doors opened. What a great job, riding up and down in a lift all day in a smart uniform!

Aunty Thelma drank a lot of Coke and took Bex powders by the truckload. No wonder she died quite young. She used to enter competitions in women's magazines and on the telly, and actually won stuff. Her pride and joy was a wrought iron and glass dining setting. I thought it was a rotten idea to have a glass-topped table — how could you get rid of brussels sprouts and other inedible stuff if everyone could see?

It was in Adelaide that we saw for the first time what television should look like, rather than the snowstorms we watched at home. It was such a change to be able to watch all of *Sea Hunt* with Lloyd Bridges, and not have to guess how the story ended. The local television presenters were treated like stars — I remember Kevin Crease and Ian Fairweather, and the beautiful Angela Stacey.

Back at Nangwarry, the latest arrival in our household was Mary, number eight, who joined Bernadette and Josephine so that the girls weren't quite the minority they once were.

7

Beachport

Just off the main street in Mount Gambier there was a used car yard called Carlin and Gazzard. The people who ran the yard must have truly been 'rev heads', because as well as the line-up of regular makes you'd see on the street every day, they'd have one or two 'rareties'. A particularly special car would be given pride of place up on a ramp under a carport type of shelter at the front of the yard. Bathed in spotlights, every bit of chrome and gleaming duco would shine! These were the days when there was no such thing as too much chrome or, as far as the Americans were concerned, too many headlights or too much tail fin.

Dad came home one day and told Mum about *the* car he had seen under the lights at Carlin and Gazzard. She didn't seem overly enthusiastic, although there was no doubt that we *needed* a new car. Quite apart from the cosmetic deterioration of the Vanguard, mostly as a result of what we kids had done to it, it was becoming increasingly unreliable, particularly in wet weather. The right-hand back door of the Vanguard didn't open, not least because the door handle had long since disappeared. We used to get in and out of the back seat by climbing through the window, even though the left-hand door operated perfectly well.

The car that had bewitched Dad was a white 1956 Ford Customline V8. No doubt about it, Dad was a 'rev head' himself. The Customline was truly beautiful, and brought 'snazzy' to yet dizzier heights. It had green leather seats and sported tail fins, albeit rudimentary ones compared to what was coming out of Detroit at the time. It made every other car on the road look ordinary — by comparison, our old black Vanguard looked like a fat cockroach. It even had a heater. We nagged Dad like mad, making ridiculous promises we couldn't possibly keep concerning future behaviour. He bought it. I could have died and gone to heaven.

To go for drives in this thing of great beauty was the ultimate thrill, especially when we were seen by other kids. We'd make out we hadn't seen them, one elbow out the window as though it was quite the most ordinary thing to be cruising around in the best car in town. At the time, the Customline was considered a large car, but it was still a bit of a squeeze for our mob. Dad was always behind the wheel, Mum would be nursing the baby, the next youngest sat between Mum and Dad, and the rest of us were wedged in the back seat. Apart from looking good, it was clearly also a very good car, and stood up well to the rigours of the savage horde which rampaged through the back seat. It survived a few years relatively unscathed, if you ignored the baling twine used to hold the back doors shut, because once again the handles had 'disappeared'. The Customline could really fly. Mum was always nagging Dad not to speed, but of course when Mum wasn't there we took every opportunity to egg him on to do 'broggies'. A broggie is performed on a somewhat slippery surface, for instance a damp yet relatively firm paddock — you didn't want to get bogged! At about twenty miles per hour, you slam on the brakes while turning the steering wheel sharply to one side. Dad wasn't bad.

* * * *

One summer while we were on holidays at Beachport, we went out to Lake George to check on the net that Dad had set the night before. Beachport was a sleepy seaside town, tucked out of the way, on a spur road off the coast road between Mount Gambier and Adelaide. Its small permanent population were fishermen from the fairly substantial crayboat fleet, or retired fishermen and farmers. There was a mixture of shacks and more substantial dwellings used as weekenders or holiday homes for farmers in the district, or people from Millicent and Mount Gambier, although people from the Mount tended to go more to Port MacDonnell.

Lake George is a very large shallow claypan, and in summer was baked hard and dry, apart from some areas which still contained water, varying from ankle to perhaps chest height. The bottom was soft and muddy under the water. Dad would walk the net out and we'd peg each end to posts we'd fashioned from scrubby branches. Although fishing was Dad's primary concern for being out on the lake, there was also the lure of the hard-baked, perfectly smooth claypan, which in some places stretched for miles — just perfect for seeing what the Customline could do. After a lot of cajoling and pleading from us, and assurances that we wouldn't breathe a word to Mum, Dad 'planted it'. It was fantastic. We topped the 'ton' — one hundred miles an hour in the old language. We were squealing with excitement at the thrill of it all, but as Dad slowed the car down the shrieks were soon silenced when we got on to some softer clay and started to slew sideways. There were a few hairy moments before Dad wrestled it under control. Driving home, he warned us again of the consequences of breathing a word to Mum, but of course the very instant we got through the door we had to blurt out in minute detail the whole thrilling event. Predictable unpleasantness followed, but for once it wasn't for me. Dad was read the riot act and told stuff like: 'It doesn't matter what you do to your stupid self, but what about the kids?' and 'When are you going to grow up?'

* * * *

Our 'shack' at Beachport had once been a sort of guesthouse. There was a reasonable sized main bedroom, a kitchen and a big living room across the front, then a number of smaller bedrooms at the back, all of which seemed to open into one another. The matchwood walls were painted cream and there was ancient lino on the floors. In a sort of lean-to at the back was a fairly rudimentary bathroom, with hot water supplied by a chip heater made of tin and shaped like a very basic rocket. I think it worked by way of cold water passing through a coil wrapped around and around the walls of the chip furnace, which then emptied straight into the tin bath. I remember there being not much you could do in terms of regulating the temperature of the water. Once the heater was stoked up and the paper lit, away it would go, vibrating and making a terrific roaring sound, spitting out scalding water into the bath through a bit of rusty pipe.

The shack stood on a fairly large block of land with a 'pit' dunny way down by the back fence. Around the perimeter of the yard, where the fence had long since disappeared, there was a thicket of blackberries. Although these were a pest in the wild, Dad would slash the brambles right back in winter time, and by the middle of summer they'd be loaded with delicious sweet fruit. We picked berries by the bucketload, and Mum would boil them up with some sugar to serve with vanilla ice-cream. When there were simply too many to cope with, she made blackberry jam.

We lived in our bathers and tee-shirts to save Mum having to spend all her time washing, and had sleeping bags for the same reason — they must have been fairly ropey by the end of summer. To take a family of eight kids and two adults to the beach for six or eight weeks, was an incredible logistical exercise. Mum would drive the car full of kids and clothes and bedding etcetera, and Dad would travel separately with the rest of the supplies in a truck or borrowed ute. Mum would stock up with whole cartons of Weetbix, tinned baked beans and spaghetti, and powdered milk. We'd often have Weetbix for breakfast, fish and chips for lunch, and if we got our way Weetbix for dinner as well. Dad always set a few craypots off the rocks, so crayfish were pretty commonplace too.

Beachport had beautiful clear water with the main beach protected by a reef. There's an extremely long jetty, which in the old days could handle the small coastal steamers which did the rounds of the little settlements dotted here and there. The crayfishermen would moor their boats in the deeper, less protected water on the other side of the jetty from the main beach. Like many South Australian coastal towns, Beachport has lots of old Norfolk Island pines, which must have been planted many years ago. Around a rocky point from the main beach is the 'back' beach, fairly exposed and not all that hospitable for swimming, and between that and the main settlement, nestled in among the scrub-covered sandhills, is the Salt Lake.

The shops in Beachport consisted of the Tea Rooms, a bakery, a butcher and a few other businesses which mainly operated only at holiday times. Across the road from the jetty was the Safcol factory, and crays from the fishing boats were wheeled on trolleys along a rail line down the length of the jetty, straight across the road and into the factory. The bakery was just over the hill from our place, so when you could smell the bread fresh out of the oven, we'd be sent to get three 'full' loaves of bread, equivalent today to six loaves of bread. The bread was difficult to cut while it was still warm, so invariably the slices would be pretty thick. Smeared with lashings of butter and piled with chunks of Dad's freshly caught crayfish, a splash of vinegar, and pepper and salt — it was heaven. If you could put a dollar value on the amount of fresh crayfish we consumed over those early sixties summers, you'd swear our name must have been Rockefeller and not Cameron.

There was a peculiar fishing by-law of the time that allowed kids, but not grown-ups, to catch crayfish of any size off the jetty using drop nets. Dad always made sure we were well kitted out! We'd head out at dusk and invariably had success. One memorable night we caught a sugar bag full, which would have been about the volume of three plastic buckets. Another night we dragged up a small carpet shark, which just happened to be swimming over the drop net as we dragged it up — that spooked us for a bit.

An old guy we called 'Uncle' Collie, who wasn't really an uncle, though he was distantly related, was retired and living in Beachport. He always used to fish from the jetty, and was really quite a 'pro', with all the right reels and rods. He had a little Austin 'Noddy' car, which was a dead giveaway. Because the jetty was so long, you could never see who was fishing out along it, but if the Noddy car was parked nearby, we knew Uncle Collie was somewhere out there to lend a hand. He probably dreaded seeing us loom up out of the dark, but he had the patience of Job, and helped not only us Camerons, but other kids as well, to untangle lines, re-bait hooks and remove some of the spookier catches. It's a wonder he had any time to do any fishing for himself, but he always seemed to go home with two or three good ones in his bag.

Uncle Gordon and Aunty Asta, who were really Dad's aunt and uncle, and thus great-aunt and great-uncle to me, had retired from their farm to a really flash white-painted house with a silver corrugated iron roof, one street back from the sea. They were loaded. They must have travelled a bit too, because their house seemed to be full of all sorts of exotic stuff from overseas. I don't know if they travelled to China, perhaps Hong Kong, but their sunroom had a lot of Chinese-looking things: vases and paintings and a black lacquered screen. Some of my grown-up relatives called Aunty Asta 'Aunty Aspro', because they reckoned she was 'hard to take'. I always thought she was okay.

Mum used to constantly tell us not to loiter in front of Aunty Asta's house waiting for handouts, because it looked 'common'. Of course that didn't stop us. We totally ignored her instructions and would blatantly lurk outside the front fence, on the off-chance she might be working in the garden, which happily she often was. Aunty Asta was quite forthcoming with funds; she'd usually give us two bob each, which of course was a fortune, and would absolutely guarantee that our appetites for sensible food would be ruined for the rest of that day.

Aunty Asta and Uncle Gordon's house was just down the road from the caravan park. If Dad had made a particularly good catch, as he often did with his net in Lake George, we'd take the fish we couldn't use to the caravan park, and flog them to the campers, three mullet for two bob. As soon as word got around that the Cameron kids were selling fish, we didn't even have to go door to door — or campsite to campsite — they'd come to us. We rarely got far past the gate before we sold out. We had to hand over the proceeds from the sales, but Dad usually gave us a bob each to spend on rotgut. Sometimes we'd tell him we had to sell the fish at reduced prices, because sales were a bit slow, and pocket an extra couple of bob. We'd then head off to the Rivoli Tea Rooms with our ill-gotten gains, and pig out on Blue Moon milkshakes and lollies.

One New Year's morning we went to gather in the net bright and early. We couldn't believe it, the net was virtually glistening with fish along its entire length. The morning was well advanced by the time we managed to retrieve all the fish from the tangle, and we eventually ended up with exactly three hundred and sixty-five fish — Mum said it was a message from God. What the message was, I'm not quite sure, unless it was the fact that we were going to make a few quid at the caravan park that morning.

* * * *

There was a picture theatre of sorts which used to open during the peak periods of summer. It was a hall really, next door to the Rivoli Tea Rooms, and the coming attractions would be advertised on posters outside the hall and in glassed-in boxes on the Post Office wall. The 'theatre' had rows of benches at the front for kids, and more comfortable canvas chairs at the back for the grown-ups, while the projectionist worked from a makeshift room at the back. When one of the film reels ran out, there'd be a short break while he laced up the next one. The break must have seemed like an eternity to the projectionist, given the boos, catcalls and whistling coming from the front benches. The projectors were incredibly noisy, and the small hall would get stiflingly hot.

A famous trick of the Cameron kids, not at all appreciated by the projectionist, was our very early version of a backward 'Mexican wave'. We'd occupy the front row of the wooden benches, then just as 'God Save the Queen' struck up, we'd simultaneously throw ourselves backwards. The domino effect was nothing short of spectacular. There'd be three or four rows of upturned benches with kids yelling and carrying on, arms and legs sticking up everywhere. Further back the grown-ups would be 'tut tutting' and making remarks about 'badly brought up children'. We soon abandoned this stunt however, fun and all as it was, after getting banned from the pictures for a week.

It was rare to have newly released films screened at the Beachport pictures, not that we would have had the faintest idea of what was new and what wasn't, unless it was a real blockbuster like

The Ten Commandments, and we sure didn't get to see that at Beachport. One of the hottest movies we saw was *Heaven Knows Mr Allison* starring Deborah Kerr and Robert Mitchum. Considering that it first hit the screens in 1957, to see it so soon as the early sixties was something of a treat. Apart from an occasional stand-out like *There's No Business Like Show Business* with Mitzi Gaynor and Marilyn Monroe, most of the features we went to see were pretty crappy, but wild horses couldn't have kept us away.

One of the worst films we ever saw was *The Gamma People*, a science fiction shocker about children being turned into homicidal maniacs which must have been made on the smell of an oily rag. Still it was sufficient to scare the living daylights out of us. The night we saw *The Gamma People* our cousin Robin happened to be staying with us for a while. The walk home from the pictures took us along a track through low scrub around a lagoon. It was a bright moonlit night, the shadows incredibly stark and the lagoon and the white clay of the track almost glowing. We were already pretty hyped up when Robin spotted some Gamma men following us, and that was the cue for unbridled hysteria. We made it home in a matter of seconds. Bright moonlit nights still give me the creeps, wondering whether the odd Gamma man is still lurking about.

* * * *

Every Boxing Day, the Rivoli Bay Regatta was held at Beachport. It was a country show, a festival, a sports day and day at the beach all rolled into one, and attracted hundreds of people from all around the district. There were marching girls in smart uniforms with their legs painted brown with fake tan, a gymnastic display, wood chopping, skiing, tagged fish, and sandcastle building competitions. One year I was positive I was going to win the sandcastle competition. I'd practised piling damp sand into my plastic beach bucket and turning it out. I knew how to make turrets and parapets, and use driftwood for flagpoles and seaweed for flags. I came up with a beauty. What I hadn't counted on was the judge's failure to recognise my ability. The judge — a lady called Mrs De Garis who was married to some dignitary or other — gave first prize to another kid. There were dark mutterings that Mrs De Garis was related to the winner, and I was consoled by the fact that Mum thought she was a 'witch', and that she 'wouldn't recognise a good sandcastle if she fell over one' — as I hoped she would!

Like any kid who holidayed at Beachport, I learned to swim in the Salt Lake. The story went that the lake was nine times saltier than the sea. I can certainly vouch for the fact that it was very salty, because if you didn't wash off with tap water after a swim you'd soon be salt encrusted. The Salt Lake was a brilliant place to learn to swim because it was virtually impossible to sink, although the water wasn't too inviting to look at, being a murky brown with dark particles floating in it. It was also quite renowned for its therapeutic qualities. Whatever the ailment, Mum was convinced that time spent in the lake would improve it, if not fix the condition outright. In my experience, it seemed she was right. Like most kids in those days, we'd develop nests of boils from time to time and, while it is true that exposing them to the salty water stung like buggery, it sure cleared them up quickly. One time Mum had an ulcer on her leg that hung on for ages. Antibiotics weren't helping at all, and it had to be constantly dressed with bandages and antiseptic. Once we got to Beachport, it took about a fortnight's worth of wading in the Salt Lake to sort the ulcer out, never to be seen again.

When it came to treating boils, a far less agreeable way than swimming in salt water was the old Antiflo routine. Antiflo was a poultice, a little like a greyish-beige plasticine to look at, and it came in a tin. The idea was to heat up the poultice between pieces of cotton gauze in the oven. Once it was nearing what seemed to be boiling point, Dad would lance the boil with a sterilised sewing needle, then slap on the gauze-covered poultice to draw out the pus. As boils invariably seemed to prefer the back of your neck or your backside, you could be guaranteed to be walking around with a stiff neck or sitting very gingerly for days.

As far as I was concerned the only downside of swimming at the Salt Lake was the walk home. Though it was only a mile or so along a dusty track winding through the coastal scrub, it always seemed to be swelteringly hot. The flies would be smothering you and, because of the amount of ultra salty water accidentally swallowed while mucking around in the water, you'd be darn near pickled, with a mouth like blotting paper. By the time we hit the old kerosene Kelvinator, the Kia-Ora Fifty Fifty went down without touching the sides.

The perils of sunburn were not as well documented in the fifties and early sixties as they are now, so each summer we'd manage a few fairly horrific burns. Mum would cover us in sun cream, but I think in those days the cream we used acted more as a basting agent than a sunscreen. When we did suffer a particularly bad burn, everyone had an old wives' tale of how to treat it. One was to smear all the affected area in butter — I think that was a bit like basting the roast *after* it was well and truly done. Another idea was cold tea, a method used a bit at our place, though I'm not sure that it worked. The most diabolical idea was a warm bath, 'to take out the heat'. Whoever dreamt that one up was a masochist: however tepid the water, anything above stone cold was agony. Occasionally as we lay on our beds barely able to move because of the burn, we'd decide we were better off sneaking out through the window and heading down to the beach. The feeling of the dark cold water on the skin was heaven. We had been warned of course about sharks feeding at night, and giant stingrays coming in close to the shore, but anything that could soothe the glowing skin was worth the risk.

The coast around Beachport was rocky and wild, and there were plenty of shallow caves and grottoes in the rocks that just begged for exploration. None of them were too deep or dangerous, but the fertile mind could run riot imagining pirate treasure and old skeletons just waiting to be discovered. To be truthful, I did not suppose the south-east coast of South Australia was nearly as rich a hunting ground as Cornwall for pirates' loot, but I had read the Famous Five and Secret Seven, so you always had to keep an eye out.

* * * *

In Beachport I first heard the Beatles. My older brother Peter bought a brand new transistor radio which he'd long been saving up for. It ran on a huge battery which cost an arm and a leg, and always seemed to need replacing, probably because the radio was always on. We'd heard about the Beatles and their phenomenal popularity in Britain, but until now hadn't actually heard their music. I remember we were standing in the kitchen at about six o'clock one evening when they came on singing 'I Want to Hold Your Hand'. I was astonished. I'd never heard anything like it in my life. Incredibly, each new Beatles song was better than the last — 'Love Me Do', 'Please Please Me', 'She Loves You'. Mum and Dad couldn't quite see what all the fuss was about, all they heard were the 'yeah, yeah, yeahs' and not much else. The Beatles focused my attention on to popular music, and I became addicted to the sound, particularly of UK artists — Billy J Kramer and the Dakotas, Gerry and the Pacemakers, the Searchers, Cilla Black and of course Dusty Springfield. I'd been vaguely aware of the Springfields and their song 'Silver Threads and Golden Needles', but when Dusty went solo and had an immediate hit with 'I Only Want To Be With You', I was hooked. All that remained was to see her in action, and soon enough there was a show one Saturday or Sunday night on ABC television featuring artists at the Hippodrome in London, and I watched Dusty sing 'You Don't Have To Say You Love Me'. I knew I was in love with all that blonde hair and black eye make-up. Here was a true goddess come to life before my very eyes — how could I ever look at another woman knowing that Dusty Springfield was out there?

* * * *

Not far from Beachport, my Uncle Jock and Aunty Julie had a farm. Jock was one of Dad's younger brothers. We were at the farm for a Cameron get-together — it must have been around Christmas time, because it was a very hot day. Uncle Mac, another of Dad's brothers, was there, with Aunty Maureen and their kids. Uncle Mac and Aunty Maureen were Presbyterian and fairly strict, and their kids were not quite as 'free range' as we were. We thought the rules for Catholics were tough enough, but the 'pressbuttons', as we called them, seemed to have it even tougher. Anyway, this particular get-together, Mum and Dad had brought a case of Passiona, which we all loved. The bottles were stacked in a fridge to get chilled, and when it was almost time to drink them, I came up with the most scathingly brilliant idea. My brothers thought so too.

We quickly guzzled down one of the bottles of Passiona without too many people seeing, and then went behind the tank stand and filled the bottle with wee. We could hardly contain ourselves with the wickedness of it all, but managed to jam the top back on the bottle and put it back into the fridge to cool off. It wasn't a perfect match for the other bottles, as far as colour goes, but if you weren't a Passiona aficionado, and Uncle Mac's kids weren't — then it was close enough. When the time came the lucky recipient was our cousin Donald, the eldest of their kids. Over the years Don copped a fairly hard time from us. He was often first on the receiving end of whatever dastardly deeds we had dreamed up.

The tops were ceremoniously ripped off a number of bottles, and we carried on as though we were mad with thirst, gulping away — and Don followed suit. His reaction was priceless, and worth the thrashing which followed as sure as night follows day. He had gulped down about half the contents of the bottle before he stopped for air, and then, in slow motion, he crumpled to the floor, alternately strangling and retching. We of course fell about with tears streaming down our faces. It was not long before things inevitably took a turn for the worse, whereupon it was very uncomfortable sitting down for quite some time.

* * * *

While we lived our early childhood years mostly oblivious to anything that wasn't in our immediate circle, the world was changing rapidly. In the ten years since my birth, George VI had died, and his eldest daughter Elizabeth had ascended the throne, the hydrogen bomb was perfected, and Joseph Stalin died. A molecular model of DNA was published for the first time, Edmund Hillary and Tenzing Norgay climbed the highest mountain on earth, and Jonas Salk began vaccinations against polio. Juan Peron was ousted in Argentina, and scores of countries became independent. The Suez crisis came and went, the Cold War was at its height and Hungary paid dearly. The Space Age began, and Castro became President of Cuba. Gary Powers was shot down in his spy plane over Russia. Top Nazi Adolph Eichmann was captured in Argentina, the Vietnam War was in its infancy, and John F Kennedy became President of the United States. The world's population also grew by more than five hundred million!

8

Beanbri

Towards the end of the time we were living at Nangwarry, there was
a bit of domestic turmoil going on at our place. I never quite
worked out what, and grown-up stuff wasn't much discussed in
front of us kids, probably because we'd blurt out our own
interpretations of it at the least appropriate moments. Dad wanted
to sell the mill to go farming. It was in his blood I think because of
his family background. There had also been some bad accidents in
the mill, and I think Mum and Dad both thought farming would
be less stressful.

So we bought a farm from one of Dad's cousins. The property
was called Beanbri and it was about halfway between Nangwarry
and Millicent, in an area known as Mount McIntyre. The nearest
town was Kalangadoo.

The farm was about five hundred acres of very flat red gum
country, with rich soil and lots of water. There were small drainage
channels crisscrossing the property and feeding into a major channel
that ran across the back. The driveway to the house from the road

was about a hundred yards long, and was referred to as 'Uncle Eric's beer garden'. Uncle Eric was an earlier owner of the property, and apparently enjoyed a tipple or two. When he gave up drinking, he had money to spare; instead of 'pissing it up against the pub wall', he bought exotic trees and shrubs during his Friday shopping trips to Millicent. The driveway was lined with these beautiful trees, spectacular at any time of the year. There were variously coloured cypresses and ornamental plums, and some especially beautiful grafted hawthorn trees by the front gate, which were a variety of colours and covered in blossom throughout the spring.

The old house, like so many farmhouses, had grown 'like Topsy'. It was no doubt originally very attractive, with verandahs right around and a high pitched iron roof. Over the years verandahs had been enclosed to make extra rooms, and it ended up like a rabbit warren, which was no bad thing when you consider that by the time we left Beanbri, there were ten kids to shelter, never mind Mum and Dad and the various 'drop ins'.

The kitchen was on the enclosed back verandah. It was a gloomy old room, with smoke-stained walls and ceiling. We cleaned off as much of the smoke and grime as we could with sugar soap, then Mum got the painters in to paint it pink, which made a massive difference. 'Pebble' or 'Bubble' vinyl was a very popular floor covering at the time, and Mum no doubt liked it, but it was not particularly practical, since the bubbles would get punctured by the stiletto heels worn by fashionable ladies. Instead we got 'cushion' vinyl, although it too succumbed to a bit of a hiding from spiky heels.

There was an Everhot slow combustion stove in the kitchen,

which also provided the hot water. Mum added a new Simpson Fabulous 300, the ultimate cooking range in 1962: it had a meat probe cooking sensor, rotisserie, pre-set cooking times and glide-out hotplates. I wouldn't have been the least bit surprised if it had also been able to 'whistle Dixie'. The only problem with the Fabulous 300 was that you needed to be an electrical engineer to work out how to use it. I think its true value for Mum lay in the fact that every woman who visited would drool over its wonderful features. Meanwhile, the slow combustion stove would burn all day and every day.

When Dad killed a sheep, all the excess fat was rendered down in Mum's big dripping pot. There was always a pot of dripping on the stove top, and it made wonderfully tasty roasts. Near the stove, in a warm place, Mum invariably had yeast growing, which she used to make 'German' cake. This was the most delicious yeast cake, almost the consistency of bread, the top of it browned with butter and sugar. Another of our favourites for an after school snack was nut loaf smeared with butter. I thought it was pretty nifty how Mum made these in old baked bean tins: when the loaves were cooked, she opened the bottom of the can with a can opener, so it was easy to slide the loaf out.

* * * *

Beanbri was basically a dairy farm, although we had some sheep and grew hay. Dad always had a spud paddock, which in the summertime had to be irrigated from the underground water which was plentiful in the area. To drive the irrigation pump, Dad had an old Field Marshall tractor, which even in those days must have been an antique. It was a huge beast of a thing, with a single cylinder motor and a chimney like a train funnel. To start it, you had to use a shotgun cartridge which went into a sleeve at the front of the motor. You then detonated the cartridge with a bash from a heavy hammer. If you started the motor in reverse, you'd have to drive the tractor around backwards, unless you wanted to start it all over again in forward. But since we only used the Field Marshall as a stationary engine to drive the pump, it didn't matter all that much. The noise it made was a long 'hoot' followed by a loud 'bang', thus its nickname, the 'hootbanger' — you could hear the Field Marshall hootbangering away from miles off.

Between the back of the house and the woolshed, there was the most wonderful old orchard, not especially productive, but like a secret garden with the trees and paths all overgrown and covered in moss and lichens. There were apples, pears, plums, peaches, apricots, oranges, lemons and quinces. Along one side a massive weeping willow thrived in the damp conditions, and along the path to the sheds, ornamental plums with glossy dark red leaves stood out vividly against the soft mauve of lilacs. Aunty Elvie used to make quince jelly, but the quince tree was a prolific bearer of fruit, and there's only so much quince jelly one woman can make.

Because of its dense coverage of large leaves, the quince was an ideal vantage point from which to shoot passing cows, sheep, dogs, cats or girls. We were not very discriminatory, however girls invariably gave the most satisfactory reaction. When I say 'shoot' I don't mean with anything particularly lethal, usually a 'spud gun' which shot bits of potato with compressed air. Like most fun things, I think spud guns got banned somewhere along the way.

Shanghais were good too, however you had to be somewhat more skilled to use them with any degree of accuracy. Some kids called them 'gings'. The easiest way to make one was with a y-shaped twig and a piece of old bicycle inner tube for the sling. The projectile could be anything. If you were really serious about inflicting some damage, you could shoot fence staples, but even for the likes of us, they were a bit on the dangerous side.

My sister Bernadette was a very unwilling target, and consequently spent a lot of her early life as our perpetual victim. Most of the time she had a runny nose, probably because she howled so much — with good reason, I frankly admit, given what we dished out to her on a regular basis. Finally, however, the worm turned, and when Bernadette's moment of glory came, I was — fortunately for me — in no way involved.

Early each morning the younger members of the family — Charles, Malcolm, Bernadette and Josephine — would walk down to the end of our driveway to catch the school bus that took them to the primary school in Mount Burr. Mount Burr was a fairly tough milling town, about halfway between our place and Millicent. On the morning of Bernadette's salvation, Charles and Malcolm were doing their usual job of making her life a misery on the walk down the drive, calling her 'Scabs'. 'Scabs' was her nickname when we were being horrible; usually she was called 'Bub'. We called her Scabs because she had very fair skin which would easily burn with the least exposure to the sun and any blister on her lips would soon turn into a nasty scab. Unsurprisingly she hated the name.

On the fateful morning, as related to me and recorded in family folklore, Malcolm and Charles were being their usual charming selves. On top of calling her Scabs, they were chucking bits of gravel at Bub. Charles was really the ringleader and Malcolm his totally willing 'yes' man. One piece of gravel apparently hit Bub on the lip, and of course copious amounts of blood gushed forth, even though the wound wasn't all that serious. All this happened just minutes before the school bus was due to arrive. Instead of dabbing her lip with her hanky, and stoically hopping on the bus as she would normally have done, Bub had clearly decided her victim days were over. Bellowing at the top of her lungs she hightailed it back up the driveway, with tears and blood spattering in her wake.

In a few minutes the bus arrived and the other three boarded. Charles and Malcolm, who fancied themselves as something of the school 'toughs', went straight down to their seats at the back, where no other kid would dare set foot. Unfortunately their 'Captains of Cool' image was about to take a serious dent. The bus driver waited a few moments because he could see a car coming down the drive at the rate of knots. In it were a cleaned up Bernadette and a feral Dad. Bernadette was placed on the bus, Dad thanked the driver for waiting, and promised he wouldn't be too much longer. He then climbed aboard the bus and hauled Charles and Malcolm out of the back seat and on to the side of the road. There, in full view of a busload of Mount Burr school kids, he took off his belt, and thrashed the living daylights out of Charles and Malcolm. It must have been a long walk back to their seats for them as they tried forlornly to muster whatever skerrick of dignity they might have remaining. Unsurprisingly, that morning marked the end of the persecution of Bernadette.

When you consider the number of beltings we copped over the

years, it's a wonder we didn't end up bitter and twisted. Perhaps we have and just don't realise it. I have to say the vast majority of thrashings we received were well and truly justified, and with a mob like ours, I truly can't imagine how we could have been kept under control at all. My sisters at least were better behaved, in their younger years anyway, and it was a rare day that any of them got a 'tap' on the backside.

* * * *

Sundays, at least for the first part of the day, were a nightmare. We'd get dressed up in our best, with our hair greased flat to our heads with Brylcreem, then climb into the car and off to Mass. I'd usually feel carsick, though the other kids reckoned my carsickness was just a ploy to get into the front seat. By this time the white Ford Customline had been traded in on something more practical, a red and white Volkswagen Microbus that was not in the least bit showy. Considering we were now an extensive tribe, I suppose the Microbus made sense, even if it was sad to see the Customline go. The Microbus had three rows of seats which in theory meant you could keep the warring factions separated to at least some degree, although in practice it just meant we had more territory to fight over.

At church, Mum and Dad, the girls and the babies would sit in one row, with Peter, Charles, Malcolm and myself directly in front of them. This meant that Dad was at a good vantage point to give us a clip around the ears for any misdemeanours. It became quite a skilled sport, to be able to provoke one of the other kids into doing something that got him a swift swipe, without copping any blame yourself. This however often brought reprisals later. Needless to say, however hard you tried to behave, your ears would be red and shoulders sore from some well-directed whacks and pinches from behind.

We used to think that Dad had eyes like a hawk, but in fact I think he hardly noticed any of the carry-on we got up to in church. It was Mum who really called the shots and issued the orders. First we'd hear the loud whisper: 'Duncan, deal out to those kids,' then came the whacks. Mum usually had three degrees of warning for us. The first was, 'Okay you kids, you're riding for a fall.' Then came, 'All right, I'm warning you kids, you're going to get the father of a hiding when Dad gets home.' And finally the big one: 'Right you kids, that's the last straw. When your father gets home he's going to flog you to within an inch of your life.' Welcome home Dad! One can only hope his days in the mill or out in the paddocks were less stressful than what faced him when he got home.

One Sunday after we'd got home and got the customary belting for our appalling behaviour both during Mass and throughout the ride home, it was decided enough was enough; it was time to fight fire with fire — we had to kill Dad. With the benefit of Peter's know-how (ignoring his spectacularly narrow escape when mucking around with electricity at Nangwarry), we had a rough idea of how electricity worked. The calf paddock alongside the house had an electric fence, and we knew not to touch that. The calves learned soon enough too. The fence was powered from a plug at the back of the shearers' quarters, and it so happened that the parking spot for the Microbus was just alongside those same quarters, right next to the fence of the calf paddock.

This memorable Sunday, we had about half an hour to put our plan into action. We had to move swiftly because we were going out to Uncle Mac and Aunty Maureen's for the afternoon. Having learned from the physics maestro that water conducted electricity beautifully and provided a solid 'earth', we flooded the ground around and under the Microbus. We then unplugged the calves' electric fence. Loosening it from the roller at one end, we wound it round and round the metal front bumper of the car. Then, just before it was time to go, making sure we were all well clear, we plugged the fence back in.

When Dad came outside yelling, 'What the hell are you kids doing? Get in the car for Gawd's sake,' we told him we couldn't because the ground was all wet and we'd make a mess in the car. Muttering away to himself about how on earth the yard could have suddenly flooded out of the blue, Dad strode over to the car and grabbed the door handle. He was flung backwards, there was a zapping sound from the shearers' quarters, and Dad ended up on his backside. We watched in dawning horror as we realised he wasn't dead. Boy, would we cop it this time. There must be a God however, because Dad thought he must have parked too close to the electric fence and the bumper had somehow entangled itself. A very narrow escape all round!

* * * *

The Microbus was the first car I learned to drive — if you could call it a car. All of us older kids knew how to drive the tractor after a fashion. Dad would set the automatic throttle on slow, and we'd steer it around the paddocks as he fed hay out to the cows. It was just as well it had a hand throttle, because our legs couldn't reach the foot accelerator, let alone the brake. Eventually we did learn to drive the tractor properly, but it was still a bit of a feat changing gears. You had to climb down off the seat in order to apply enough pressure on the clutch, then nip back up onto the seat, with the other leg at full stretch to reach the accelerator pedal. Like most farm kids I suppose we could drive by the time we were ten or eleven.

Though not exactly sporty, the Microbus was terrific to learn to drive in. Because of the boxy design of the vehicle, with the controls right up front and the motor and gearbox right at the back, it had what was called a 'forward control' system. This meant the response of the gear change was rather vague and 'slushy', but at the same time very forgiving — so that some of an inexperienced driver's less than smooth moments were disguised to a certain degree. It was also not particularly powerful, and the steering was a bit vague; altogether perfect for a beginner.

I was fascinated by cars, and it was too bad the Microbus was not the sort of vehicle you wanted to show off about. In fact we didn't want to be seen in it at all, especially by kids whose folks had something a bit sleeker, and virtually every car on the road fitted that category. Some of our uncles had nice cars. Uncle Allen had a Holden Premier and Uncle Murray had a Humber Super Snipe, which even though it had twin headlights, a nice wooden dashboard and leather seats, wasn't particularly cool, because it was Pommy.

Mama Cameron had a blue late 1940s Ford Anglia with rear doors that opened backwards. When she got her brand new Mini, green with push button start on the floor and as modern as a beehive hairdo, the old Anglia was left on our farm. We loved it. Despite being threatened to within an inch of our lives, the moment Mum and Dad went out, we'd take the Anglia down to the back of the farm near the big drain and do broggies. If we were particularly daring, we'd see how far we could get it up on two wheels before it rolled over.

On one memorable occasion when we were busy impressing cousins who were visiting from Melbourne, we actually got it to roll twice, although we were aided in this by a happily placed embankment. It says something about the way cars must have been built in the forties that it didn't suffer as much as a dent. We were always careful to clean off any grass or mud before Mum and Dad got home, and when we broke a headlight by misjudging a gate we told Dad a cow had bunted it — I'm not sure what shower we thought he'd come down in.

* * * *

Dad's cousin Angus, from whom he'd bought the farm, sometimes helped out at spud time. He used to smoke. So did Dad when he was offered one. He'd point out to us that it wasn't necessary to tell Mum everything, usually at about the same time he'd allow us to have a drive of the Land Rover, and miraculously, I don't think we ever did dob him in. Considering Mum had eyes in the back of her head, and a nose that could smell a rat under three feet of cement, I think she must have just turned a blind eye.

* * * *

Most of our weekly shopping was done at the little town of Kalangadoo, about seven miles from Beanbri. The grocery store there was a Farmers Union co-operative, and the people used to serve from behind the counter, with all the goods stacked on shelves behind them. I used to love ringing the order through to the store in the morning so that when we went into Kalangadoo in the afternoon, our order would be stacked ready in a heap of boxes. Any really big shopping, like stocking up on all the supplies to last over summer at Beachport, was done in Mount Gambier where Moran and Catos was a genuine true to life supermarket, just like the ones you saw on television in the United States — right down to the huge brown paper bags to take the groceries home in.

When we went to Beachport for the summer it was a real pain to be rostered on to help shift the irrigation pipes in the spud paddock. Dad and Peter did most of the work, but occasionally Charles and myself, being next in line as far as age goes, would have to help. Invariably the weather would be sweltering, and all you could think about was the rest of the mob having a good time at the beach. Peter by now had turned sixteen and had his driver's licence. He had saved furiously and bought a smoke-grey Mini, and had an Astor Diamond Dot radio fitted in a cradle beneath its virtually nonexistent dash. There were one or two compensations if we had to go back to the farm to help with watering the spuds. One was the fact that if Dad wasn't around, Peter would let us drive an old Land Rover which Dad had bought at a government surplus auction.

One summer when I was fourteen we were hooning around in the spud paddock when the driver's door flew open just as we were going through a gate (it had a bit of a dicky latch). The Land Rover's skin was aluminium, and when the door panel hit the protruding spindle of the lock on the gate, it not surprisingly ripped through the aluminium like a can opener. The tear in the door ran almost its full width, and was about two inches wide. We knew we'd be in for it if Dad found out, so we had to do some very quick thinking.

When Dad came home to water the spuds himself two days later, he must have been taken aback at the number of 'very willing' volunteers. We draped some spud bags over the door of the Land Rover, as well as a pile in the back. Had he asked why, we'd planned to tell him we thought it might be a good idea to stockpile a few bags in the paddock to save having to do that job later on. As it happened, he didn't ask.

'You can drive, Champ,' Dad said.

'No, it's okay, you drive,' I replied, and that surely should have been enough for him to smell a rat, because normally I'd have run over hot coals to have a drive of anything. I sat in the back of the Land Rover, immediately behind Dad, and as we swung through the gate, Peter distracted him saying, 'Look over there at that!' God knows what he was supposed to be looking at, but it did the trick. Dad was distracted long enough for me to slip the catch on the Land Rover's door, and fling it open as hard as I could. It hit the gate post with a hell of a whack, ripping off the spud bags as it did so to reveal the terrible gash sustained two days previously. When Dad pulled up, we all climbed out of the Land Rover and stood there in amazement. Dad scratched his head. 'Gawd, you wouldn't read about it,' he said.

Because of the low lying nature of the countryside around Beanbri, there was an abundance of water, which would form swamps right into the summer months. This was an ideal habitat for snakes, and unfortunately all of the species in our area were poisonous to a greater or lesser degree. There were tiger snakes, copperheads, black snakes and brown snakes. Mostly they would keep out of your way, but there were always exceptions. They were particularly active at the beginning of summer when they ended their hibernation and were mating.

There were all sorts of tales circulating about the best way of killing snakes. With lots of small children about the place, snakes were unwelcome anywhere near the house or garden, so they'd get dispatched fairly unceremoniously. It seemed the most effective and humane method was with three strands of fairly heavy gauge fencing wire twisted together into about a six-foot length. This gave you a bit of leeway, in that you didn't have to be too near the snake when you gave it a whack. The idea was to break the snake's back, killing it virtually instantly. We were also told never to approach a snake from behind, because they could strike at you by flinging themselves over backwards. I never tested the theory. A popular method, especially with women, was to fling a pan of boiling water over them — a fairly ghastly thought, but effective. I imagine that women on isolated farms felt they had to do something to protect their families, because if a child was bitten, the chances of getting to hospital on time were fairly remote.

Fortunately, being cold-blooded creatures, snakes were really only active over the heat of summer. In the depths of one winter at Beanbri we brought a barrow-load of wood up to the wood box at the back door. The wood heap was a bit further down the drive towards the sheds and the idea of the wood box was to give the wood a chance to dry out a bit from what seemed like a perpetual winter drizzle, before bringing it in for the stove or the open fire. Unwittingly, we'd carried a hibernating black snake in this barrow-load, coiled up in a hollowed out log. At some point in the afternoon, Mum went out to the wood box, picked up the said log, and threw it onto the lounge-room fire.

The snake soon de-hibernated, if there is such an expression, and very quickly slid out of the fire, across the carpet and under the lounge. Babies, toddlers and kids were all evacuated in very short order, boiling water was employed, and the black snake came to a gruesome end.

Dad used to constantly warn us to stay away from the main drainage channel at the back of the property. In winter it was dangerous because of the torrent of water which swept along it, and in summer it was even more perilous because snakes would breed in the rabbit burrows along its banks. They would sun themselves and mate in the sandy entrances to the abandoned burrows, where they were a relatively easy target for hunters, especially in the very early summer while they were still a little sluggish.

Telling a young teenager, 'don't go near the drain' was like saying 'go to the drain immediately.' If something was out of bounds, it was exciting. Some blokes who used to work for Dad in the timber mill used to make pocket money from selling snake skins, so we figured we could be rolling in dosh in a matter of weeks, given the number of snakes we knew were lurking in easy reach along the drain.

Our chosen weapon was the old-fashioned straight spring rabbit trap. We didn't of course set the trap, because who had ever heard of catching a snake in a rabbit trap? Instead we held the trap by the pin, by which we could swing it using the chain to get some speed up for the main part of the trap, which served as a club. It was amazingly effective. The idea, at least in theory, was to sneak up over the side of the drain bank, careful not to cause undue vibrations of the earth which would alert the snakes, or they'd be straight off down the burrow. If you were very fortunate, you would catch the snake unawares, basking in the burrow entrance, then 'whacko!'

My first foray, with my cousin Damien from down the road, was a stunning success. We dispatched five snakes, which we hung over the handle of a long shovel for the journey home. Fortunately, Mum and Dad were in town for the day, so we could proceed unhindered with our ghastly plan. Having seen some of the mill workers skinning snakes to sell the skins, we knew what a tedious and specialised job that was, so we decided we needed an easier way of doing the job.

Mum had a Simpson washing machine with an electric wringer which you could swing away from its position over the machine tub if you wanted to wring out clothes over a trough. My brilliant idea was to chop off the snake's head and then feed the body through the wringer, tail first at maximum tension, so that all its innards and spooky bits would simply fall out of the open end where the head used to be. It seemed to me the idea was sound, but like all great innovations, this one obviously needed a certain amount of refinement which, unfortunately, we never did get around to given the disaster which followed.

We started the wringer going, and fed the snake into it tail first. So far so good. But instead of the innards oozing out like sausage meat from its skin, the bulk of the snake refused to go through the rollers. It blew out into a great bulge and then burst, sending snake blood and guts flying everywhere, on the walls, the ceiling, the floor. The laundry was like something out of a horror movie, and those of us unlucky enough to be in the vicinity looked like victims of a mad slasher. The remaining snakes were quickly buried behind the wood pile, and the rest of a perfectly good day was wasted trying to clean up the mess before Mum got home.

* * * *

It was while we were living at Beanbri that possibly the single most important event of my entire life occurred — though I had no idea of its import at the time — and it was my father who brought it about. Dad occasionally went to clearing sales around the district, held by farmers who were selling up for one reason or another. They were a popular way of getting rid of a lot of machinery as well as the junk that inevitably built up over the years in one big sale. Dad would come home with boxes of knick-knacks that 'just might come in handy one day', except that most of the stuff ended up stored away in the back of our shed, only to appear again at our own clearing sale.

The best buy of Dad's life, the one that would affect my future, was a pile of boxes crammed full of books. There were books of all descriptions, hundreds upon hundreds of them ranging from classics to medical journals to kids' books. Suddenly I had the complete Famous Five, Secret Seven and Ten Again stories, and heaps of Biggles books, many of which I'd already heard in serial form on the radio, but which were so much better in book form, where you could devour the story in one go, with no missing bits. There were also some very peculiar old volumes of *Cole's Funny Picture Book*, with quaint old-fashioned stories and puzzles, and weird cartoons, like kids getting belted across the backside by a caning machine powered by a bloke pedalling a bike-like contraption.

Fortuitously, we had floor to ceiling bookshelves on either side of the big old stone fireplace in the living room, and I took it upon myself to catalogue all the books, number them, and set up a 'library' on the shelves. I gradually worked my way through the books, starting with *Anne of Green Gables*, *Anne of Avonlea* and *Little Women*, and a stack of Dickens' novels, of which *Great Expectations* was my favourite. These were all quite easy to read, but as I got towards some of the more 'grown-up' books, the going got tougher. I couldn't for the life of me work out what James Joyce's *Ulysses* was on about.

9

Not the 'F' Word

Being predominantly a dairy farm, the bulk of the work at Beanbri revolved around the milking of the cows and the maintenance of the herd. Dad built a state of the art 'herringbone' dairy. This was very modern at the time, and there were very few of them around the south-east at all. In the old style of dairy, the cows would be driven head first into a 'bail', where their heads were held in position with a wooden pole while they were milked. In our herringbone dairy, the cows were driven in seven to a side, where they would stand on an angle, facing away from the persons doing the milking, so that their udders were easily got at. The farmer works in a 'pit' running down the centre or 'backbone' of the herringbone configuration, so that the udders are virtually at waist level, precluding the need for constant bending over. A great idea in theory and, in most cases, in practice.

As the seven cows on one side were being milked, another seven would be moved on to the opposite platform to have their teats washed in preparation for milking. As the first lot were done you'd swing the machines across, connect them up to the second lot, and repeat the performance until all the cows had been done. Even with milking seven cows at a time this could be a lengthy process, with herds often exceeding a hundred cows.

One minor drawback of the herringbone system was the positioning of the farmer in the pit, below and behind up to fourteen cows at a time. This could be fraught with danger, especially if the animals were a little 'skitterish', as was common. 'Having the skitters' was Dad's expression for diarrhoea. On a few occasions Dad did manage to be in precisely the wrong place at the wrong time, with hilarious results — at least from an onlooker's viewpoint. On a frosty winter morning he presented quite a sight, trudging up from the cowshed through the orchard trailing wafts of steam from his head to toe 'coating' — at least it was warm, he said!

We had among the herd some favourites. Violet was a very old Friesian cow whose udder was so big it would sometimes drag in the mud. She surely was the Dolly Parton of the bovine world. Dad decided to measure how much milk she gave one day, and she overfilled the four gallon bucket. She may not have had the same quality milk as the Jersey or Guernsey cows, but she made up for it in quantity. Another of the cows was called Nelson, because she only had one eye. I'm not sure it was a very good idea to give the cows names, because it made it much more difficult for everyone if they became ill or 'had to go'. Nelson was one of those; she became very crook with some ailment, and had to be 'put down'. Dad was not very good at 'putting down'.

Farming at the best of times is not for the faint-hearted, and a dairy farm is no exception. Most of the newborn calves are taken from their mothers and sent off to slaughter; only the very few 'lucky' ones are kept to rear as milkers themselves. One terrible season, a bout of spontaneous abortion swept through the district, and a lot of the cows were losing their unborn calves. Some of the 'new Australians' from the milling towns, never ones to waste anything, would gain the farmer's permission to go among the herd and would virtually catch the aborted calves before they hit the ground. We considered the idea too gross to think about, but the tender white veal was apparently a great delicacy.

The few 'lucky' calves that were to be reared to become milkers, still of course had to be taken from their mothers. It was our job to feed the 'poddies' as they were called, and any town kids who happened to visit our farm at poddy feeding time would be green with envy, they were so cute. But when you had to feed them morning and night, seven days a week, their cuteness wore off somewhat. I think the most we fed at any one time was around twenty, and that was a handful. We gave them a manufactured powdered milk called Denkavit, which smelled terrific when you mixed it up with warm water. The aroma was deceptive, however. I took a sip once, and it tasted like liquid fish, but at least the poddies loved it.

If a calf had only just been separated from its mother, we sometimes had to teach it to suck. To do this we'd dip our fingers into their bucket of milk, then put our fingers in their mouths until they got the hang of sucking, which they generally picked up very quickly. Gradually they'd follow our fingers down into the bucket and in a matter of seconds would be slurping the milk down.

Dad eventually bought a contraption called a 'Calfeteria' which was a quite scathingly brilliant device. It consisted of a very large bucket into which you tipped the calves' formula; around the sides teats stuck out, with plastic hoses going down to the bottom of the bucket. Although it was an excellent idea in theory, in practice some of the calves were natural gutses while others were more reticent when it came to feeding time. While the greedy gutses were getting the lion's share of the formula, some were missing out. Dad solved this by setting the teats into a fence along one side of the sheep pens in the shearing shed, with individual buckets of formula lined up along the other side of the fence. Some of the gutses would still wolf down their share and then try to bunt the slower ones off their teats, but at least you could sort that out and it was a lot easier to police. Thereafter poddy feeding generally passed without incident, apart from one dreadful night when, thank God, it wasn't my turn on duty.

It was shearing season, and the shearers were due to arrive first thing the next day. Whether or not the shearers' impending arrival had any bearing on the decision they made is immaterial, because for whatever reason, Charles and Malcolm, whose turn it was, decided to leave the poddies in the sheep pens overnight. Unfortunately, in their hurry to be done with the evening feed, they neglected to fasten the gates between the shearing deck and the holding pens where the poddies were accommodated at feed times. During the night, the calves pushed open the unlocked gates and cavorted all over the shearing deck. Whilst cavorting, they also pooed everywhere, making the entire floor a rink of slippery green poo. When the shearers arrived bright and early the next morning, they were confronted with an entire shearing shed covered in poddy poo. Shearers being the picky creatures they are, they took a very dim view indeed.

The first I became aware of this was at about five thirty when I was woken up by cries of anguish and frustration as Dad laid into Charles and Malcolm with a hose from the poddies' feeders. 'You bloody hopeless, paralysed piss ants,' he was yelling. I'd rarely heard him so riled, and I'm sure Charles and Malcolm weren't enjoying the 'good morning' call. But for once I wasn't on the receiving end, so I feigned sleep and thanked my lucky stars.

One winter an epidemic of the skitters really decimated the calf population. Once they caught the bug, you couldn't stop the calves shitting, and they'd eventually waste away and die. We tried all sorts of stuff from the vet, but nothing seemed to have any effect. Then Dad heard of an old wives' tale about dropping a red hot coal into the calf's milk bucket. Whether this was responsible, or whether the disease was naturally on the wane, I suppose we'll never know, but things did improve after that, and old wives' tales have to have some basis in fact to get handed on I suppose.

* * * *

We didn't have too many sheep at Beanbri, just a small flock to breed fat lambs. Lambs were sometimes abandoned by their mothers and other times their mother may have died. Either way, we'd often place baby lambs on bags in front of the slow combustion stove, trying to revive them. A teaspoon of brandy proved amazing in cases where you might have sworn the lamb was dead. It wasn't always easy to get the lamb to take to a bottle, but it did work out more often than not. Once a lamb had revived sufficiently — usually after a couple of days — Dad would try to match it up with a ewe which had lost a lamb of her own. Working on the idea that animals recognised their own scent, Dad would spray the ewe's nose with hairspray, then spray the orphan lamb all over with the same spray: amazingly it seemed to work in most cases.

One spectacular failure was a lamb we called Nimmy because of the sound she made drinking from her bottle. She refused to be fostered, and we ended up raising her ourselves. She remained very friendly, and in fact I don't think she ever understood that she was a sheep. When she was an adult, she never mixed with the other sheep, and at milking times when Dad rounded up the herd, Nimmy would lead all the cows in to the dairy. Whenever we were mucking around in the tall grass which covered the farm in springtime, Nimmy would follow us around. She made a great pillow to lie back on when she was sleeping and we were feeling lazy in the sun.

* * * *

The old orchard at Beanbri was such a good playground, it was inevitably the scene of much mischief and misadventure. The weeping willows were not only great for climbing around in, you could make great bows from their bendy branches. It was in the orchard that Peter got bitten on the neck by Joe the horse. He was standing under the quince tree when it happened, and we reckoned that old Joe, who was a bit blind, mistook his neck for a quince. After that I decided that if I was going to get bitten by a horse, the neck was the last place I'd want it to be. Well, almost the last.

One of the scourges of the orchard were the possums. They loved the fruit as much as we did, even more perhaps, and would feast monumentally on all the different fruits as they ripened, or in some cases just before they ripened. Not that anyone begrudged the possums a little fruit, it's just that they didn't play fair. After possums had virtually decimated what had promised to be a particularly good crop of pears, Dad had had enough. On this fateful night, when someone yelled that they'd spotted a possum, he went for his gun. In the boot cupboard just outside the back door, he kept a double-barrelled shotgun, ostensibly for disposing of the snakes and rabbits we had in plague proportions.

Between the back door and the edge of the orchard was a very high limestone tank stand. Being made of stone, the room beneath the tank was always lovely and cool, and Dad used it to store meat that he'd freshly killed. The offending possum was sitting high up on the tank stand, clutching a pear firmly between its paws. Dad quickly loaded the shotgun, and with great excitement we gathered behind him as he stepped out to take aim. Someone shone a torch up on to the tank stand to mesmerise the possum, but the beam revealed one very small catch. Squatting right alongside the mother possum, and so small we hadn't seen it at first, was a baby possum. The mother possum was taking tiny nips out of the pear and delicately passing them across to her baby. Needless to say the shotgun was put away with Dad muttering, 'I'd probably have shot a hole in the tank anyway.'

At the top of the orchard, just past the clothesline was an old outside toilet. Mum and Dad had a new toilet installed inside, just off the laundry, but with a family our size, you couldn't have too many loos, so the one outside wasn't decommissioned. This was the ideal place should you happen to be suffering from constipation; at least you could suffer in peace, rather than face a procession of people banging anxiously on the door. I must say, constipation was especially frustrating if there were visiting kids whom you'd far rather be mucking around with instead of sitting in the toilet wriggling and sweating. I heard a riddle at school which I could readily identify with. Question: What's the definition of constipation? Answer: Teethmarks in the toilet door!

At the other end of the alimentary scale were infrequent bouts of the trots, as we termed diarrhoea in our house. Mum's standard remedy was an invention of the devil called Kaomagma. This vile concoction came in a tall, brown, rectangular bottle. It appeared an innocent enough white liquid, with the consistency of runny cream, however the moment it hit your mouth it turned into bitter chalk, virtually impossible to swallow. We detested it. The way it dried out your mouth and throat, it amazed me that it didn't turn your whole body into a statue.

Dad apparently *hadn't* been dosing himself up with Kaomagma. One very entertaining morning, a few of us were sitting up in the haystack across the drive from the orchard, while Dad was cleaning up the cowshed after the morning milking. We watched him come belting out of the shed, running towards the house as if the place was on fire, before settling into an ungainly sprint, all the while grappling with the stud fasteners on the front of his overalls. About a quarter of the way up the orchard path, his sprint changed more to the action of an Olympic walking champion. About halfway to the house he became very stiff legged and looked for all the world like he was trying to clutch a bunch of flowers between his bum cheeks. In the final quarter of the journey, which must have seemed an eternity to him, Dad adopted a much more relaxed if slightly bow-legged gait until finally he reached the back porch yelling, 'Mel! Come and get the hose!'

Although it wasn't obvious to me at the time, much of our life at Beanbri was centred around the orchard. I suppose that was because of the way it was centrally located, with the infrastructure of the farm fanning out around it. At the bottom edge of the orchard, right against the woolshed, was a large chookyard. Chooks can be quite characters, and we had some interesting occupants in the chookyard over the years. There were a couple of particularly nasty roosters in succession, but they didn't last long once they'd attacked Mum. Dad reckoned roosters were no good to eat because they had balls, and balls made them taste funny. That must have been why we had to castrate male lambs and calves, so that when they grew up to be wethers and steers, they'd taste okay. I didn't know how Dad knew that roosters had balls, because you sure couldn't see them. Dozing off to sleep with my mind wandering in all directions, I wondered if cannibals cut the balls off missionaries before they ate them.

We had quite a few adventures with chooks. My cousin Damien, who lived on the farm across the road from Beanbri, told us that chooks were really easy to get drunk, because their brains were so small they were almost nonexistent. I doubted that theory, but in the interests of science, we decided to experiment anyway. Damien nicked a half bottle of his Dad's scotch, and brought it over to our farm one weekend. We mixed the scotch with the chook's bran and pollard and tipped it into their feeding troughs. I think we had thirty or forty chooks at the time.

So far, this was our most successful experiment ever, until of course it all went horribly horribly wrong. It seemed like the chooks got plastered in seconds. They were staggering all over the yard and constantly falling over. We were howling with laughter; this had to be the funniest thing I'd ever seen. Then ominously, after a few minutes, the chooks began to fall asleep. Trouble was, they weren't asleep, or the 'sleep' was of a very permanent nature: they were stone cold dead!

Damien bolted. We panicked and washed out the feeding troughs to destroy the evidence, although you could still detect the smell of scotch in the air. When we drew Dad's attention to the fact that something really weird had gone on in the chookyard he went to investigate. After his initial amazement, he came back up to the house scratching his head, saying to Mum, 'Gawd Mel, you wouldn't read about it. The whole ruddy lot of the chooks have carked it. There must be some vicious chook bot doing the rounds.'

On the other side of the orchard from the driveway was a row of densely planted cypress trees which formed an impenetrable barrier. They had originally been a hedge, probably to serve as a windbreak to protect the orchard, but over many years had grown out of control and developed into quite large trees. The branches were so dense, it was easy to build forts and hideouts with very little, if any, chance of being spotted by the enemy — for enemy, read grown-ups or siblings who weren't part of this particular operation. It was in our cypress fort that Robin and I hatched the plot for what was to be the crowning triumph of our early careers.

Dad was never a man for much profanity, but this day we surely tested him. A near neighbour at Beanbri (not Damien's dad) had a fetish for blowing up things with sticks of gelignite. He mainly restricted his explosive exploits to old red gum stumps and that sort of thing, but we reckoned he must have had quite an arsenal at his place. What we required was a piece of the slow burning fuse that he regularly used. It burned internally, and you could work out how long it would take to set the explosive off by the length of fuse you used.

With rat cunning, I managed to relieve our neighbour of about fifteen feet of fuse from the back of his toolshed. The temptation to look around for a stray stick of gelignite was enormous, but even I had enough sense to know that perhaps that would be taking things too far. Anyway, Robin already had the explosives, in this case four eight-penny bungers saved up from Guy Fawkes Night.

The plan was to strap the eight-penny bungers together with sticky tape, connect their wicks to the fuse we'd 'borrowed', and then bury the device about six inches deep in the middle of the lane which ran between the cypress trees and the bull paddock. Dad would drive the cows to the dairy along this lane, after they'd spent the day in what we called the 'house paddock'. He was milking about seventy cows at the time, which meant the lane would be nearly full of cows from end to end, so the 'bomb' had to be placed exactly halfway along its length. The fuse would be concealed just below the surface until it reached the trees. This was simple enough to do, since there was no grass at all in the lane, what with the amount of traffic over it with cows coming and going. Once we'd buried the bungers and laid out the fuse, no one could have guessed what lay beneath; it was virtually undetectable.

There wasn't enough fuse to do an experimental test, so we just had to trust that we'd covered all the contingencies. Come milking time, Robin and I were ensconced in the cypress trees. Robin had a pair of old binoculars. Off in the distance, you could hear Dad whistling the dogs as they rounded up the herd and guided them towards the laneway. We were beside ourselves with excitement as the enemy approached. It really was an idyllic scene on a fine, still, late afternoon. As the cows slowly converged on the lane, we could see Dad well behind, ambling along with the dogs, chewing on a piece of straw as was his habit and keeping an eye out for stragglers. This was his routine for almost every day of the year, and nothing would have seemed out of the ordinary.

When the first cows entered the race this was our signal to light the fuse. I was sick with anticipation as we waited for what seemed an eternity. The lane was almost full from end to end when we started to think we'd failed. Perhaps one of the cows had kicked the fuse free, or maybe it had just malfunctioned. Then, all hell broke loose.

The first surprise was that instead of one massive explosion, there were four loud individual bangs, like old-fashioned shotguns being fired off in quick succession. We nearly fell out of the tree from the shock of it, having by now given the bungers up as a failure. This was better than any cracker night had ever been, and it was still broad daylight. From then on, everything seemed to slip into slow motion. The cows, of course, bolted, and no two seemed to head off in the same direction. Some burst through the fence into the bulls' paddock, some leapt through the impenetrable cypress hedge into the orchard, some went back the way they had come, while others sprinted straight past the cowshed and into the far distance. The one thing they all shared in common was the fact they had gone berserk with panic. Milk was spraying from every udder even as they bolted.

Within seconds there wasn't a cow to be seen within a hundred yards. Darkie, one of the dogs, having somehow survived the stampede, had flattened himself onto the ground, doing a good impression of a smallish black and white bearskin rug. His eyes had disappeared completely, having rolled back into his head, leaving only the whites showing. I'd always suspected that Darkie was at least slightly deranged, and I'm darned sure this little episode didn't help his psychological condition one bit.

I've deliberately not mentioned my father's reaction till this point, however I don't think it would be too much to say that this was one of the pivotal points in his life. One of those moments when one is tested so severely that one can only choose between two options: crack up completely and succumb to hysteria, or use the experience as a sort of tempering of the steel — a moment to draw from inner resources strengths you didn't know you possessed, knowing that having survived this, you can survive anything life might throw at you in future.

Dad's reaction was neither of these — or perhaps it was both. Sure, he did crack up, and in a fairly frightening fashion, but he recovered almost immediately. Still in slow motion, Dad raised both his hands in the air, his fists clenched so tightly we could see the whites of his knuckles. We could see the whites of his eyes, for that matter — he was a good match for the dog. It was at about this point that I started to have some misgivings about what we'd thought was such a scathingly brilliant idea. As we watched, Dad sank slowly to his knees, slumping forward on to his hands as he did so. There on the ground, from the pit of his stomach, he started bellowing.

'Those f—ing kids! I'll f—ing kill them! Dear God if I don't f—ing kill them, I'll go hopping to f—ing hell in a f—ing hand cart!' While he was yelling this he was clawing at the ground, snatching up handfuls of dirt and slowly letting it trickle through his fingers. There, before our shocked gaze, Robin and I watched a man literally foaming at the mouth. This was not looking good.

Alerted by the explosions, and no doubt the sound of a stampede followed by the bellowing, both bovine and human, Mum came belting out of the house yelling at the top of her lungs, 'Duncan, Duncan, not the 'f' word, Duncan.' By now, quite a mob had gathered to see what all the fuss was about. Robin and I were highly chuffed, if a little overwhelmed, at the success of it all. For once everything went as planned, and as usual the downright stupidity and recklessness of what we had done dawned on us approximately one minute too late. This was not really what we'd had in mind at all. But, sadly, there's no way of winding back time to do things differently, and what we *did* have in mind, I'm not really sure; I only knew it wasn't this. Needless to say the cows didn't settle down for days, and it took Dad at least as long. Robin got sent back to the Mount, I got belted.

10

Marist Brothers, 1963

My primary school days had ended at Our Lady of the Pines in Nangwarry. Peter had already headed off to boarding school at Marist Brothers College in Mount Gambier and it looked like I was headed that way too. Although Mount Gambier was little more than a half hour drive from our farm, it was not practical to attend the college as a day student because the only school bus to pass our farm went to Mount Burr and Millicent. So boarder it had to be. As a kid who really was a homebody, the idea didn't thrill me one little bit, even if my older brother was going to be there.

Getting kitted out for boarding school was a very big deal because it meant a heap of new clothes, even if they were clothes you wouldn't be seen dead in outside of school. There were some hand me downs from Peter, like the disgusting dark blue school blazer with light blue piping. At last I was allowed to wear long pants, and that at least seemed grown up. The uniform pants were of grey melange, presumably called 'melange', because the fabric was a mixture of natural and synthetic fibres. However long you

The front of the administration area at MBC.

had them, the grey melange daks never lost their 'itch', which was of course much worse in the warmer months. To complete the outfit, shiny white shirts, containing not a skerrick of natural fibre and capable of generating enough electricity to light a house. This was the age of nylon and bri-nylon, and any other variation of synthetic material the petrochemical industry could come up with.

Thank God that by the early sixties, braces weren't really fashionable anymore. Come to think of it, neither were the totally ridiculous hats we had to wear as part of the MBC uniform. It was a beanie sort of thing with a peak on the front. When you have been born with a 'boof head' — which is to say a head just ever so slightly out of proportion to the rest of the body, and all my family had been blessed with those — and these stupid hats were designed for pinheads, the end result was even more bizarre. Worse, all the rellies, especially the older ones, kept telling me I looked 'very smart'. That was enough to set the alarm bells ringing in any self-respecting kid's head.

As the name would suggest, the college was run by an order of religious men called the Marist Brothers. They were a motley collection, with a heap of problems. A few of them were all right, but over the next three years of my life, I was to see and experience all types of psychotic, neurotic and downright weird behaviour from these so called 'religious' brothers.

For all the reasons I had admired the Brown Joeys, it seemed the Marists were the very opposite. Perhaps it was just the difference between the sexes, but where the nuns had been strict, their methods appeared to be based on fairness and compassion. With the Marists some of their behaviour was downright sadistic, at best just 'odd'.

MBC was an agricultural college, set on a small farm on the slopes of the volcanic system of Mount Gambier. The farm was on the outskirts of town, about a mile further around the crater from the hospital where I was born. The sports field — what was to be the scene of many long hours of misery and torture for me — was called 'The Flat'. It was really the bottom of a crater from a blowhole at the time when the area was volcanically active. For years the military, or army cadets, had used the Flat as a rifle range, firing across the open space into the side of the Sugar Loaf, an extremely steep-sided hill forming part of the decaying caldera around the lakes. Further beyond the Sugar Loaf was Mount Gambier itself, the highest section of the caldera, with a stone lookout on top which resembled a single turret from a medieval castle. The slopes on the outside of the crater to the top of the Mount are covered in pine trees. At night you could lie in bed in the dormitory and listen to the wind roaring through the pines. Sometimes the roar was comforting, mostly it was lonely.

At the entrance to the college was an ornate stone and iron arch. Through the arch was a long driveway lined with cypress and Norfolk Island pines. Checking-in time for the boarders at the start of first term was all day Sunday. Kids who'd had to travel hundreds of miles were at the school first thing in the morning, poor buggers. For some of them it must have been dreadful, not knowing another single soul in the place. At least I had my brother there. Peter and I always got along, he was my older brother after all, but he was more mature for his years than I was, and vastly more responsible. My best mate remained my partner in crime Robin, who was a day boy, so for the first weeks there, in the hours before classes began and after the day kids went home, apart from Peter, I was on my own. The other boarders might as well have been from Mars; I didn't know any of them. Because he'd already been at college for a couple of years before me, Peter had his own group of mates. I soon discovered there's only so much 'hanging around' even a very tolerant older brother can put up with.

Some kids howled as their parents left, which I thought was pretty bad form; mind you it wasn't a patch on the bad form I subsequently came to display when my family left after their

Sunday afternoon visits. This was some months into my 'sentence' after I'd discovered what utter utter bastards some of the Marist Brothers were. I'd beg, plead, scream, entreat — threaten to fling myself under the wheels of the Microbus — I'd do anything to get out of there, and I didn't care who saw or heard my little performances.

It was a motley old intake in 1963. Some kids came from the Eyre Peninsula, which was a hell of a long way away. They were usually farm kids being sent to Agricultural College to set them up for life on the land. During the summer break, a couple of the Brothers, no doubt the least weird of them, would do a recruiting drive around the state; the Eyre Peninsula and the west coast must have been fairly rich pickings.

A whole swag of kids came from the western districts of Victoria, no doubt because it was so close, just across the border. The kids from Victoria were a bit funny, and had different names for things as basic as a kit bag — they'd call it a 'port' — and in words like 'school' and 'pool' they emphasised the 'oo'. In fact I'd have said they all spoke like Bert Newton, if I'd heard of Bert Newton at the time.

There was a kid from Darwin called Felix Mullen. God knows why he was sent all the way from Darwin, although mind you, if my parents had called me Felix, I'd probably have wanted to move as far away as possible too. There was even a kid from Fiji, whose name I've forgotten — we always called him Fiji. His folks must have been expats because he didn't look the remotest bit like a South Sea Islander; he was fat and white with flaming red hair. He was persecuted something shocking by one of the more odious Marist Brothers, who saw him as a particularly fine bullying target.

The one bright spot on an otherwise extremely bleak horizon was the presence of my cousin Robin, even if he was only a 'day scrag'. Robin's family still lived in Mount Gambier, so it would have been a bit odd had they sent him to board — although I bet it passed through their minds from time to time. Robin and I ended up in the same class together, though the teachers did display the good sense early on to keep us as far apart as possible.

Kevin Fidler, one of the Victorian kids, eventually became one of my best mates; he came from a place called Merino and, like me, had an older brother already boarding at the college. He was a small neat kid, with a peculiarly shaped head — long, and sort of flat on the sides. Fidler used gallons of Texan hair grooming liquid which, as I've already mentioned, set like a helmet when it dried. I used to think that should we suddenly have a meteor shower, Fidler would be the only kid not knocked unconscious.

* * * *

When motor cars are the central focus of your life, they become a sort of yardstick against which years and events are remembered. I will never forget, for instance, the ride in Allen Longbotham's Austin Healey 1962, or Uncle Glen's Chevy, which seemed to have been on the scene for as long as I could remember. In 1963 the Marist Brothers had a new EJ Holden Special, while we still had the red and white Microbus — which had not grown any 'cooler' over the years. Uncle Glen finally traded his old Chev in on an FE Holden. It was in beautiful condition, and in fact would have been an object of great envy *except* for the fact that the paint job was in three colours. At that time one colour was okay; two colours, very smart indeed, but three colours — that was one colour too far. The pink flash down the side was the offending bit, but still, it was a lot less embarrassing than being seen in a red and white Microbus crammed full of kids.

One family at the college had a Rambler Classic, which was quite a sensation; another had a maroon Humber Super Snipe, which would have been a lot cooler had it been American and sported some chrome or at least a couple of fins. The first of the Valiants, the slope-backed 'R' series, were appearing, and they were definitely okay, especially if they had the push button automatic gear change on the dashboard, which was just about the most space-age thing I'd seen since my mum's Simpson Fabulous 300 stove.

One of the lay teachers at the college was called Mr Durning, although we had to call him 'Sir'. He was single and lived at the school, and I think in later years he might have actually become a Marist Brother. He would have fitted in well: he looked just like the rest of them, only dressed in 'civvies'. He was an unsmiling fellow who always seemed to be looking for a reason to admonish someone. For some reason 'Sir' was on yard duties a lot. He had a Vauxhall Victor sedan, the one with the horizontal tail lights rather than the vertical fins. It was a stodgy looking thing, and you could actually stop it running by stuffing stale cake or spuds up its exhaust pipe.

Stuffing foodstuffs up the exhaust of a Vauxhall Victor is not as easy as it sounds; the operation has to be worked out with military precision, especially when the enemy and their informers are everywhere. The refectory where we ate our meals was to be the source of the ammo. When some special event on the Church calendar was being celebrated, we'd be treated to a 'feast', which signified the same crappy old food, but with cool drink and stale cake thrown in. Two or three pieces of stale cake would clog up the Victor beautifully, so we'd wait for a feast day.

Smuggling the cake out under our jumpers was no problem; it's not as if it would crumble apart. The main risk was the cake dropping out and breaking a toe. With a few strategic lookouts, jamming it up the exhaust wasn't difficult either. The next thing was to make sure you were in the vicinity when 'Sir' tried to start the Victor. It would wind away for ages, until the bits of cake flew out all over the quadrangle, or the engine flooded. The colour of 'Sir's' face after such an event was something to behold. We were hanging out for him to burst a carotid artery, but unfortunately he never did.

From time to time we inmates were rostered for 'spud duty', peeling spuds in the kitchen for about ninety hungry boarders plus the Brothers and other staff. That meant a lot of spuds. Luckily, they had a fairly efficient machine for the job, a sort of tumbling device. You'd throw a bucket of spuds in and most of the skin would get knocked off them. Then you'd just have to cut out the eyes and the bits of peel that had been missed before slicing them up. Then it was over to the cooks to transform them into some culinary surprise — usually mashed with lumps, or mashed with *more* lumps. The good thing about spud duty of course was the free access to spuds, just the ticket when there was a prissy Vauxhall Victor itching to have a spud or two jammed up its Khyber.

When you've managed to pull off a prank like the jammed exhaust, there's no real fun in it unless other kids know, so they might make the appropriate admiring comments. Unfortunately, there's always a snitch or two in any mob, and it wasn't long before the names Cameron, Mullen and Fidler were being mentioned in connection with the persecution of the Vauxhall. A fair cop is a fair cop, but when someone put a heap of sugar into the petrol tank of the Brothers' new lemon and white EH Holden Special with the 179 motor, and the suspicion instantly fell on us — that was an outrage. The fact is, we had nothing to do with it. I was full of admiration for whoever it was had come up with so scathingly brilliant an idea, but I was not so keen on carrying the rap for it, which involved copping 'six of the best' from one of the sadists.

* * * *

In the refectory, eight kids were allocated to each table with a table 'head' who was supposed to keep the rest under control. There was quite a bit of jockeying to get on to the table of one of the better 'heads', because most of them were bossy pieces of work from the more senior ranks. Anyone who so much as suggested that perhaps they might be thinking of a 'vocation' to become a Marist Brother when they graduated could be assured of a 'head' boy posting.

At breakfast time two huge cans of milk would be set down at one end of the room, and immediately grace was out of the way, the sprint was on to be first to the cans. A thoughtful kid would mix the milk before pouring any into their jugs, because overnight the milk would settle and the cream would have risen to the top.

At our school thoughtful kids were fairly scarce, and it was first in best dressed. The fastest to the cans would meticulously scoop all the cream from the top. Back at the table this would be poured over porridge or Weeties. There were enough pimples at the college to keep Clearasil in business until the millennium.

Next came the soggy toast with Vegemite or jam, and if you hadn't brought your own Vegemite from home, it was just soggy toast and jam. The jam came in square four-gallon tins, and the story got around that it was made from rotten pumpkins, with sugar and food colouring thrown in for the apricot variety, and lots of crappy red fruit of indeterminate origin for the red variety. It was even said that rats sometimes ventured into the pumpkin mincer, and thus got pulverised into the jam. The fact that there was no evidence of fur or bones in the jam didn't occur to me, but it was about this time that I decided peanut butter was the safest bet. I couldn't believe my ears when some kids told me what was in Vegemite, and I went off that too for a while, though not for long.

The big dormitory at Marist Brothers was a huge room on the first floor of a barn-like building. There were three rows of old iron army surplus beds; a row along each side of the room and one down the centre. The bedding was old grey army blankets, with threadbare blue cotton covers, which were hell to get the wrinkles out of when you made the bed each morning.

Each boy had a half wardrobe and cupboard alongside his bed in which to keep clothes and personal belongings. Shoes were always a worry; like the Glo-Weave Graduate shirts, the popular shoes at the time could not be accused of harbouring a single natural fibre. They were as synthetic as synthetic could get, and as a result, if you had a problem with sweaty feet, you had a *real* problem. By the end of a warm day, the odour emanating from your shoes could have dropped a water buffalo at fifty paces. Multiply that fragrance by sixty or seventy pairs, and I think you'll get my drift.

All over the world the Beatles were starting to influence the way kids looked and dressed, which wasn't such a bad thing given some of the other fads of the early sixties, like fluorescent socks. Pink, green, yellow, you name it, the brighter the better; so bright they'd almost glow in the dark, and, once again, not a natural fibre to be found. These of course were banned immediately from Marist Brothers, as were Beatle haircuts and pointy toed shoes. On Saturdays we were allowed to wear some civilian clothes, like jeans, provided they weren't too tight and trendy, and white socks — quite a look really. If we happened to be going into town to a movie, we had the riot act read to us about the dire consequences of 'bringing disgrace upon the college' — in fact, even the most minor misdemeanour, like jaywalking or talking to girls, could be construed as 'bringing disgrace upon the college'. In retrospect, considering how I schemed and plotted constantly to get out of the college, it is a wonder I didn't deliberately invite expulsion. In fact, it never really crossed my mind. I think getting expelled would have upset my parents too much, and despite my resentment at being sent to college in the first place, I didn't want to do that.

* * * *

About once a month the boarders were allowed a so-called 'free' weekend, which meant we were allowed to go home on Friday afternoon, to be returned to the lock-up on either Sunday afternoon or Monday morning. Kids who lived too far away, like those from Fiji, Darwin or the Eyre Peninsula, stayed with friends or had to remain at the college — I used to feel sorry for those poor wretches. I'd beg Mum and Dad to let me stay home until Monday morning, even though it was extremely inconvenient for them, what with the cows to milk and the other kids to get off to school. One particular weekend it rained continually, and all the roads to Mount Gambier were under water. It looked as though it was going to be a couple of days at least before the floods subsided. Unfortunately the road to Kalangadoo was not flooded quite so badly, and the Adelaide train ran through there on the way to the Mount, so onto it I was bundled. We didn't get to travel on a train very often, so at least that was exciting. It was freezing cold, and the only heating on the train, at least in 'cattle class' where I was travelling, was from canvas-covered drums that heated up when you shook them. The drums were about two feet long and oval in cross section; when not in use they were stored under the seats. I have no idea how they worked, but work they did; the more vigorously you shook them, the warmer they got. They must have been filled with some very spooky chemical indeed.

The Mount Gambier show weekend always caused something of a dilemma. Of course our college, being an agricultural college, naturally encouraged its students to make the most of the opportunities provided to inspect the very latest in agricultural machinery and equipment, the very best produce, and the elite livestock from all the surrounding districts — all on display at the one showground. Unfortunately at the very same showground were other attractions of a less agrarian but far more compelling nature!

The show was one of those occasions when full school uniform was compulsory, after all we were 'representing the college'. This was none too subtle a code for: 'You kids put one highly polished shoe wrong, and punishment of the most unimaginable sort this side of Hell awaits.' Before show week we'd be lectured incessantly about what to look out for: a very fine pig which had won a ribbon in Adelaide, a particularly productive dairy cow, an exotic chook, or perhaps the very latest Massey Ferguson tractor with free pamphlets for our school projects. 'Tractor schmactor,' was what I thought; most of us couldn't have given the proverbial rat's about the latest agricultural innovation. Like every other kid in Australia, the object of my attention was the noisy, smelly, trashy and downright sinful sideshow alley.

About the only educational exhibit that was remotely interesting was a display featuring the Australian Space Program at Woomera one year. They had an actual rocket, or at least a model of a rocket, the 'Blue Streak' I think it was called. There was heaps of information on what the Americans were doing in the space race, but precious little on the Russians. I suppose that wasn't really surprising, after all, the Russians were communists, and they had the nerve to get into space first. Anyway, we'd belt through the sensible exhibits like demented things, grabbing samples and pamphlets as evidence, just in case we got quizzed later.

Then it was into the toilets to rendezvous with my cousin Robin who would have brought me a change of clothes in his bag. In my civvies I could melt into the crowd and stand somewhat less of a chance of bringing the school 'into disgrace'. Only the boarders had to wear uniform; I suppose the Brothers thought that whilst we were their responsibility we had to look and behave our best.

Then it was a case of where to start? Every year the show got better. There were all my favourite rides: the chair-o-plane — basically, metal tractor seats on chains that would fling you out at right angles as the whirlygig thing in the centre started to rotate — the octopus, the ferris wheel, bumper cars and real petrol-engined go-karts. And the food — now this was *real* food — deep-fried hot dogs, fairy floss and toffee apples. Real doughnuts, the ball-shaped ones, deep-fried as you watched then rolled in spiced sugar and pumped full of hot raspberry jam. Drinks in every colour under the sun and ice-cream confections which defied gravity (and the digestive system), and more rocky road and honeycomb than you could eat in a lifetime.

Some of the newer rides had space-age names like Orbiter and Gravitron. It was the Gravitron that brought me undone in 1964. It was essentially a large wire cage and you were strapped on to the inner wall of it. Then the machine would start spinning, getting faster and faster until you felt like you were being crushed through the wire wall, and your face was sliding off. Then it would start to go up and down as well, it was wild. When I was eventually released, I fell onto the grass and retched up all the rotgut I'd stuffed down to that point. In between waves of nausea and vomit attacks, I remember thinking 'this has to be the best day of my life'.

When I'd recovered sufficiently it was time to check out the tent shows — keeping an eye out for any of the Brothers who might be loitering about the place. Sometimes they got into civvies to blend in with the crowd, but you could always spot them a mile off; they were the blokes in the slightly daggy clothes that might have been conservatively trendy a few years before. While most of the young blokes of the day had discovered Beatle haircuts, the younger Brothers (who always got 'Show Duty') had the short back and sides.

There was a Country and Western show starring brother and sister team Ricky and Tammy, and a guy who was very good at cracking whips. With his stock whip he even cut a cigarette in half, while a girl assistant was smoking it. Some kids reckoned that Ricky and Tammy weren't really brother and sister, but only pretended to be because they were travelling around Australia together all the time, and they weren't married. There were some really bad performers in the Country and Western Show, but at least Ricky and Tammy were all right, even though everyone looked a bit grubby. Over the years my mum had drummed it into us that all show people were a bit that way, 'a bit common' was her expression.

Out the front of the Jimmy Sharman boxing tent there'd be a guy in a dressing-gown bashing away on a big bass drum, inviting all comers to take on their troupe of boxers to win 'twenty quid'. I wasn't really interested in the boxing, I never could see the sense in two blokes belting the crap out of each other for no reason other than the entertainment of the crowd. Judging from the numbers queued up outside the tent, however, I was clearly out of kilter with public opinion.

The Haunted House was another matter altogether. Most years there were a couple of Haunted Houses, and word soon got around about which one was best. Invariably, that became the one with the biggest line-up outside. An especially good Haunted House had the lot: skeletons, ghosts that glowed in the dark, a graveyard that smelled of what was supposed to be rotting corpses, although I think they just let off a stink bomb from time to time. Best of all were the electric shocks. Passing through rubbery curtains you'd get a low voltage 'jolt' which these days I'm sure would be highly illegal. I can just imagine the number of people with dodgy tickers lining up for compensation, though when I think about it, I don't recall ever seeing an old person going into the Haunted House — for 'old' read anyone over twenty.

There was a tent which featured a variety show with boring singing and dancing until it got to the good bit, where a lady got sawn in half on a sawbench. The circular saw was huge, like the ones Dad used to have in the mill, and extremely noisy. Even so you could still hear the lady screaming as she was sawn in half, with strange coloured blood going everywhere. I thought it was a bit odd that she could keep screaming after she'd been sawn completely in two, though Robin reckoned it was because she was cut below the lungs.

The undisputed highlight of the 1963 Mount Gambier Agricultural Show was Vanessa the Undresser: 'Ladeees and Gennermen — DI-rect from the YOU-Nited States of America — the Queen of the Steamy South — Miss Vanessa Lee from Tennessee!' The spruiker out the front didn't need to do much encouraging, the gaudy painting on the front of the stripper's tent said it all — and more. Depicted was the most voluptuous woman we'd ever seen, knockers even bigger than my mum's. At least that's what the painting suggested. Robin bought the tickets, because although he wasn't any bigger than I was, he looked more mature. Being a 'town kid', he was also definitely more streetwise — even though we couldn't have told you what 'streetwise' meant.

The first part of the show was very boring. For some unknown reason, the audience consisted entirely of blokes, or, to be more precise, kids my age or a little older trying desperately to look cool and a smattering of old 'pervs'. The clientele failed to appreciate the Dance of the Seven Veils, which comprised some 'quite common' looking girls parading around in bathers with flimsy veils wrapped around them.

Little better was the ubiquitous Las Vegas routine with the same girls wearing heaps of feathers stuck on their backsides and heads. The sequinned bathers were so brief that they disappeared up their bottoms, or at least they appeared to, and my mind was starting to wander along these lines, when the lights dimmed and a hush came over the tent. There was a repeat of the spiel we'd heard outside and then a spotlight came on and, to the sound of stripper music — gosh it didn't get much more common than this — Miss Vanessa Lee from Tennessee sashayed onto the stage.

She was covered in glittering bits and buried under the feathers of what seemed like a dozen ostriches. She was mesmerising. She also must have been sweltering. I couldn't believe the number of layers of clothes a woman could discard before she got anywhere near the interesting bits. It seemed like forever, though it was probably less than ten minutes, but eventually she got down to business. The stage was strewn with piles of feathers and sequins, and filmy bits and pieces — long gloves, girdles, things I'd never seen before. The climax of the show consisted of Miss Lee striking a grand pose in a pair of flashy, but very modest, bikinis. The spotlight went off and it was all over, to the sound of polite clapping and a few of the old pervs yelling, 'Get it orf, get it orf.'

The fact that Vanessa Lee from Tennessee was more likely Shirley Smith from Footscray, who was probably the wrong side of forty, *and* had had a lamington or two too many over the years, was of little concern to us. As far as we were concerned, Vanessa Lee was all woman, and was the topic of conversation around the college for weeks. The rest of the show was quite dull after Vanessa — not even the crappy trinkets in glass cabinets, that you paid a bob a go to have a try at snaring with a mechanical arm, could divert me.

11

Self Abuse

Despite the fact that there were girls at home, they were not at all interesting to me, I suppose because they were sisters, and of course much younger. At Marist Brothers we were effectively shut off from those mysterious creatures called girls, and thus they became all the more fascinating. Fascinating?! Until this point, girls had been the 'enemy' — shocking 'dobbers' and 'tale tellers', the cause of many a whacking. But I was fourteen now, and the hormones were kicking in. There were some females on the staff at the college, mainly in the kitchen, but they were well and truly over the hill — they were even older than my mum.

Once a year, the older inmates were allowed to go to an extremely heavily policed social with the girls from Mater Christi College. For this important event, when you wanted desperately to be attractive, standards of dress for both girls and boys came under even closer scrutiny than usual — anything too trendy was *out*. Sometimes the arbiters of taste could be caught out, being unaware of a particular fashion trend, but as soon as they got the picture —

look out! Pointy toed shoes, for instance, proliferated around the college for weeks until one of the brothers caught on, and of course they were then banned immediately.

For weeks before the social the whole school was harangued about how 'young gentlemen' behaved in front of 'young ladies'. There was to be no dancing too close, and definitely no touching, other than hands. Nothing, in fact, that could in any way, shape or form, bring disgrace upon the school. We'd all heard stories about how boys would polish their shoes to such an extent they were effectively mirrors, so they could look up girls' dresses. I think the Brothers must have heard those stories too, because this was one of the very rare occasions when the polishing of shoes wasn't policed with the normal rectitude. Once the social was on there was nothing much to get excited about, or so I was told, just a dreary old-fashioned band banging away, and a heap of awkward kids standing around feeling sheepish. I didn't last long enough at school to actually experience a 'social' for myself, so I had to rely on hearsay.

Around this time Gene Pitney was enjoying a string of hits. 'Only Love Can Break a Heart' stuck in my mind because it was so melancholy. It suited my mood at Marist Brothers perfectly. Not that we were allowed to listen to 'modern' music all that often. Some older kids were permitted to have transistor radios and could listen to them on the weekends. Kevin Fidler's older brother Ian had one, so occasionally we'd get to hear the latest hits on that.

* * * *

Fidler and I sometimes climbed into the huge bales of paper in the machinery shed to play with our willies. The paper was to be recycled in Adelaide, with the proceeds going to the overseas missions, and some of the material that came in — surplus and out of date magazines from newsagents in town — made particularly interesting reading. *Man* was my favourite magazine, with heaps of what my mum would call 'bold hussies' posing shamelessly in various stages of undress. In retrospect it was not all that graphic, but shocking enough at the time, and the inspiration for a fair amount of 'willy playing'. If you were ever caught with 'filthy' material like *Man*, you could easily be expelled.

The Brothers had a term for playing with your willy. We called it 'wanking', but that expression was banned. The 'correct' term was 'self abuse', and the Brothers warned us constantly of its dangers: self abuse could become addictive (they were right about that); your brain gradually became enfeebled (they were possibly right about that too); when you grew up and married you probably wouldn't be able to have children because you'd 'wasted' yourself, and you'd gradually lose your eyesight, etcetera. It was scary stuff. We were also told that self abuse was a sin and had to be confessed. The first time I confessed to self abuse, the priest in the confessional was very intrigued and asked me for all sorts of details. I couldn't understand why he needed to know all the gory bits, and could only suppose he needed them in order to work out the appropriate penance.

I used to worry a lot about wanking, just in case there *was* a shred of truth in what the Brothers were telling us. I didn't fancy the idea of going blind, and I certainly didn't fancy the idea of not having kids of my own when I grew up. I wasn't all that partial either to the prospect of spending eternity in the everlasting fires of hell with all the other tortured souls who had no doubt abused themselves. For three whole days I went without a wank, keeping my mind on higher things as we had been told to do, using the lives of the saints as edifying examples. The trouble was, the saints were all out of the Middle Ages, and there didn't seem to be any point of contact between their lives and mine. I was in turmoil.

Then I had my first wet dream. I couldn't believe it! There I was, being as pious as I could, and my willy seemed to be telling me it had a mind of its own. I went to the chapel to pray for guidance (as we'd been exhorted to do). I didn't want to go blind, on the other hand surely just a little bit of self abuse once in a while couldn't be all that wrong. I set a test for the Virgin Mary. There was a statue of her in the College Chapel. If she wanted me to give up self abuse, she'd give me a sign by moving. I prayed intensely and waited five minutes. She didn't move. I'd never been more pleased in my life.

It was around this time that Dusty Springfield became a big fixation for me. She was the personification of all that was glamorous and sexy and tasteful. I heard on the radio that she had gone to a Catholic school and was still friendly with the nuns who had taught her — I wondered what they thought about her. Mum said the way she wore her hair all teased up, and the way she 'piled on' the make-up, made her look a 'bit common', though before long she changed her tune on that.

One Sunday, on a free day from jail for me, Mum and Dad picked me up and we all went to visit Uncle Allen and Aunty

The coolest milk bar in town was Donovans'.
Not only did they make milkshakes and the thickest of thick shakes, they also
had 'Coke and Sars' and 'Coke and Raspberry' — an icy cold bottle of Coke
tipped into sarsaparilla or raspberry syrup.

Phyllis and their daughters Maxine, Diane and Meredith. Uncle
Allen now had a Holden HD Premier Automatic. It was a
wonderful car, even if Holden did replace it very quickly with the
HR, which squared off the pointy fins at the front. The word
around at the time was that they'd had to change them as
pedestrians were getting impaled on the fronts of HDs. Anyway,
my three cousins all had the Dusty Springfield 'look' and I

pointedly asked Mum if she thought they looked 'common'. She gave me a look that would make bread go stale, and said, 'No, they look quite smart and modern.' To top it off, Mum herself went through a red duffle coat, stiletto heels and Dusty Springfield hair stage, although to her credit, she never caved in to the mascara to Dusty's extent.

When we saw the Dusty at the Hippodrome special on television, I was in love. She wore a long glittering dress and I was mesmerised. Here was Dusty at the peak of what she described as her 'French Model' look, with so much mascara she looked a bit like a panda. Mum said she looked like someone had 'punched her in both eyes.' I thought she looked fantastic.

The Harrap girls with their Dusty look were as cool as you got in Mount Gambier. Peter used to hang around with them a lot, especially after he left school and got his Mini. My cousin Meredith taught me the finer arts of how to 'pash' in the back seat of Uncle Allen's Premier. She reckoned that girls liked boys who kissed a certain way, and that if I wanted any chance whatsoever with girls, I had to learn to do it right. Girls didn't like boys who tried to check their tonsils out, or boys who tried to suffocate them. Nor did they like boys who smoked, because kissing them was like 'licking out an ashtray'. It didn't strike me as at all odd that the girls used to light up a fag themselves from time to time. I was very glad of the lessons, though I think in truth my cousins enjoyed pashing with Peter more than me, even though they told me I was 'sweet'. You can't begin to imagine how insulting it is to a fourteen-year-old boy to be told he's 'sweet'.

* * * *

The farm side of the Agricultural College was run by a bloke called Brother Brian. He was all right. Some of the brothers, I think, were perhaps not bright enough to teach, so they did other things. There was a Brother Cassius who was a carpenter. He spent ages and ages making new beds for the dormitories, not before time mind you. The beds he made had slide out cupboards underneath, and were a vast improvement on the old army surplus cots. Brother Cassius was all right too, he was a very quiet fellow. We used to speculate on what sort of life these two guys had before they became Marist Brothers — they seemed to be quite regular fellows who wouldn't be out of place in a regular family, unlike some of the weirdos who wouldn't fit anywhere.

We boarders were rostered to help with the various farm duties: milk the cows, feed the pigs, clean up the pig pens, and so on. Brother Brian must have shuddered when he saw I was rostered on to help in the cowshed. Handling animals was not my strong suit, and the mechanics of the milking machines were a complete mystery to me — a mystery I never managed to solve — although I was reasonably good at scrubbing the stainless steel vanes from the cream separator. Brother Brian had a radio in the dairy, so that was a plus. There was also a gas copper which was good to stand by on freezing nights. Brother Brian used to swear from time to time, which we thought was a real hoot. No doubt he was well and truly driven to the occasional profanity. He also knew some vulgar little ditties.

Little birdie flying high
Dropped a message from the sky
It landed in the farmer's eye
Thank the Lord that cows don't fly.

Just alongside the dairy, in the machinery shed, there was an old 'Furphy' water cart. Moulded into the iron on the back of the cart were the words: 'Good better best, never let it rest, until your good is better, and your better best.' I thought that was really clever, and would have made a very good school motto.

When it came to the farm roster, I particularly hated pig duty, mainly because you could never get rid of the smell. It seemed to permeate everything, and you could smell pigs on your hands even after you'd showered and scrubbed yourself raw. Also I was a bit scared of them, especially sows with new litters, and the grouchy old bugger of a boar.

* * * *

Some kids got up to stuff which would have been 'right up my alley', except that I wouldn't find out about it until it was over. There's a distinct disadvantage in not being able to be in a dozen places at once. When I heard about the tale which follows I was furious, because I would have been in it up to my eyeballs given half a chance.

One night, under cover of darkness, a group of kids rolled an old corrugated iron rainwater tank most of the way up the Sugar Loaf — no mean feat in itself. Quite often kids would take old car tyres

Looking down on MBC from the Sugar Loaf.
Farm buildings and chem lab to the left of the main building, the flat —
our sports ground — to the right.

up there, because to watch them roll down was spectacular. Bouncing over the ridges on the way down, they'd sometimes go incredible distances into the air. If some poor unsuspecting bystander had one land on them, it would have been curtains for sure. Anyway, the kids managed to get the tank about two thirds of the way up the hill, climbed inside, and let it rip. Fortunately for them, most were flung out almost immediately, but one of the Victorian kids stayed in the tank for most of the descent. No show ride ever devised could have been a patch on the rainwater tank as it careened down the hill. When they recovered the sobbing mess near the bottom of the hill he looked like he'd fallen into a giant spud peeler. Miraculously, despite being bruised and battered almost beyond recognition, nothing was broken. No one ever attempted the rainwater tank stunt again.

* * * *

In the big mound and trench at the bottom of the Sugar Loaf, at one end of the Flat which served as our sports ground, Robin and I dug a fort. The mound had been used as the target area when the ground was a rifle range, so there were heaps of spent bullets everywhere. We dug a tunnel into the mound for a distance of about five or six feet, then hollowed out a 'room'. We supported the 'ceiling' with bits of wood and corrugated iron, but it was no doubt still terribly dangerous. Our 'gang' were the only kids who knew about it, and we hid the entrance with a pile of rubbish so it wasn't obvious to any passers-by. Inevitably, of course, one of our gang defected and some of the other toughs in the school took over the fort, but as usual Robin came to the rescue with yet another of his breathtakingly brilliant ideas.

One Saturday afternoon Robin and I worked out a rendezvous in the Oaks, as they were called, an old stand of oak trees growing up the hill along one side of the Flat. Robin brought with him our secret 'equipment', in this case a great big fat eight-penny bunger. As always, Robin was well stocked when it came to pyrotechnics and cracker night explosives.

We waited until all the toughs were in the hideout they'd snatched off us before we struck. Some of them were obviously smoking in there, because you could see smoke wafting out of the concealed entrance. Creeping down to the opening from above, Robin lit the wick on the bunger. I was terrified he was going to blow his fingers off, because he held on to it till the last possible moment. I needn't have worried, because by now he was very experienced in these matters. With just a second or two to spare he flung the bunger down the tunnel then belted back up the slope. From where I stood, all you could hear was a muffled 'thump' followed by a belch of smoke from the entry tunnel. Then there were the screams, which were followed by a stream of kids emerging from the entrance, eyes watering, covered in dirt and soot and bits of cracker wrapping. They were clutching at their ears and looking around them trying to work out what had happened. We should have hightailed it immediately, because you didn't have to be Einstein to work out what had gone on. After the few moments it took them to recover, they laid into us and bashed the living daylights out of us — another of those bashings which was well worth the pain!

12

Bastards in Black

Like many kids who went through the Catholic education system, I had fleetingly thought that it might be a good life to be a priest or a brother. But God in his mysterious ways soon sorted me out of those foolish notions by allowing me to experience the Marist Brothers. From being an average to reasonably bright student at Our Lady of the Pines under the tutelage of the Brown Joeys, I hit the wall in a big way. From my first year at Marist Brothers, I loathed most of the brothers with a passion, and no doubt the feeling was reciprocated.

But not all the brothers were out-and-out bastards, some of the younger blokes were just fine, especially a couple who had just come out of the novitiate. I'm sure one of them at least was gay, even though at that time the word 'gay' had an entirely different meaning. But unfortunately the bad eggs taint the lot. One particularly nasty brute went by the name of Brother Adrian. One of his less endearing traits was playing what he called 'double or quits'.

He'd pose a question concerning the subject in hand and if you should get it wrong, you had the chance to go for 'double or quits'. This meant taking a chance on getting the next question right, or get a double caning. Invariably I'd get the answer wrong, and stupidly 'double' until I had to take 'six of the best'.

Brother Adrian loved wielding the cane, and very often the blood would seep through our swollen fingertips where he had thrashed us. He was a little man with ratty features and slicked down hair and it probably bugged him rather badly that he was shorter than a lot of the kids in the school. Still, he had a very big cane, and that must have made him feel good.

Latin came a close second after maths in the contest for which subject I hated most. I could see no possible use for learning that agricola was Latin for farmer, and nauta for sailor. So what? Farmer and sailor were good enough for me, and besides, no one on earth still spoke Latin. I wrote in the front of my Latin textbook: 'Latin is a dead language, as dead as dead can be — it killed the Roman Empire, and now it's killing me.'

Brother Raymond was another lovely piece of work, short, fat, ruddy faced, and always a bit grubby looking. His particular pleasure was humiliation. He loved to pick on fat kids and gave Fiji a shocking time. Fiji wasn't the brightest match in the pack, and Brother Raymond easily sussed that out. He would make Fiji stand up, then ask him a question. When he got it wrong, he'd make him stand at the front of the class and ridicule him. With his bright red hair and extremely pale skin, Fiji would blush very easily. There the poor devil would be, standing in front of the class, trembling with fear, and bright crimson with embarrassment. But that wasn't enough humiliation for Brother Raymond. He'd taunt him until he cried, saying, 'Just look at you, fat boy, all sweaty. You're sweating like a pig, fat boy.' One day, I couldn't help myself, and mumbled loud enough for a few kids around me to hear, 'He's not nearly as fat as you, Fat Guts.'

Fat Guts was what we all called Brother Raymond behind his back. The kids who heard my comment tried to stifle their giggles, but not of course before Brother Raymond noticed. Immediately he yelled out, 'All right Mister Cameron, you're obviously the school comedian today. Why don't you come out to the front and share it with the whole class.' As I walked to the front, I thought poor old Fiji was going to flake out, he'd gone from crimson to deathly white, and was trembling all over. Even before I got to the front of the class, I'd made up my mind what I was going to do. I stood on the teacher's platform alongside Fiji as Brother Raymond bellowed at me, 'Okay funny boy, out with it. What's so amusing?'

I was just about flaking out myself with fright, but in a voice as loud and clear as I could muster I said, 'Fiji might be fat, but he's not half as fat as you, Fat Guts.' You could have heard the proverbial pin drop. No one laughed this time. Fat Guts exploded, raining blows down on me and knocking me to the floor where he gave me a couple of kicks for good measure. I really hoped he'd have a heart attack, but he didn't. I was pretty sore and sorry for myself for days, but it was another of those occasions where the pain was well worth it.

* * * *

I ended up being sent to the Principal's office on about six occasions, interestingly enough, *not* for calling Brother Raymond Fat Guts. I think he knew himself that he'd gone too far when he went berserk with his cane, and rather awkward questions might have been asked.

To get sent to the Principal's office meant you were really in for it. Generally this was for brawling or breaking school property or some such, when you could expect six of the best. While I was at Marist Brothers there were a couple of principals — Brother Bertinus who was really odd and Brother Aidan who was quite a decent fellow. How Brother Aidan and his real-life sibling, Brother Walter, ended up with this crew I could never work out. If you were unlucky enough to be sent to the office for corporal punishment, the worst part was the waiting that preceded the lecture and subsequent caning. Strangely enough, I don't believe either Brother Aidan or Brother Bertinus got any pleasure from belting kids, unlike some of the others.

Brother Bertinus was a sad looking little bloke, quite skinny, with a huge red hooked nose covered in lots of little blue veins. On a couple of occasions, just before lights out in the dormitory, I was called to his office — not to be punished, but to see if I was 'developing properly'. He gave me a little speech about how important it was that boys my age were 'developing properly'. If everything wasn't happening naturally, then he could get a doctor to 'help things along'. He'd then slip his hand into the front of my pyjamas and fondle my penis and testicles. All I could think about was his heavy breathing and his horrible red nose covered in blue veins. This wasn't the fun 'mucking about' that Fidler and I sometimes did, this was terrifying. After a while he'd stop, and tell me everything was coming along just fine, and that there was no need to tell anyone else about his 'check', because this was all about growing up. It sure was!

* * * *

The shower ritual at the college was positively Dickensian. Hot water came from an old industrial boiler and the showers were located in a big tin shed across the quadrangle and two tennis courts from the main college buildings. At the entrance to the shower shed was a shallow bath of Condy's crystals, which we had to traipse through to avoid what we referred to as 'foot rot'. Foot rot was really any spooky diseases of the feet, like tinea or the papilloma wart virus. The foot rot bath stained your feet a bright yellow colour, so all the boarders wandered around with what looked like severely jaundiced feet. There were about twelve showers in open cubicles along one wall of the shed. The showers nearest to the boiler room were in great demand; these were the ones where the water would be hottest and the pressure strongest. The further you distanced yourself from the boiler, the grimmer it got, especially in mid winter when the weather was freezing.

We'd queue up outside the shower shed, where we be allowed in twenty-four at a time. The first twelve got straight into the showers, while the others would strip off, wrap themselves in their towels, and wait for the brother to clap his hands or blow the whistle to signify the changeover, then the sprint was on for the best showers. The most embarrassing thing to happen at this stage of course would be to get a 'stiffy' in the shower. This happened to kids quite often, although in my case it didn't matter much because I was still 'developing'. Nevertheless, I avoided thinking about Dusty Springfield in the showers, just in case. There was a kid from near Adelaide called David Zimmerman who really *was* developed, but it didn't seem to bother him; I think he enjoyed showing off. The kids who were 'developed' had to wear a jockstrap playing football, or a box playing cricket. Some of the kids definitely wore them for pose value, because they needed such accessories no more than I did.

* * * *

Although we'd been warned continuously, first by the nuns, and then by the brothers and the priest, about the dangers of 'testing God', the temptation was too great. After all the stories we'd been filled with about heroic saints and miracles in the history of the church, I was busting for a miracle to occur, even if it was of a minor nature. I especially liked the stories of Saint Francis of Assisi and Saint Teresa of Avila. I reckoned if a miracle were to occur, they'd be the ones behind it.

The categorisation of sins was causing no end of bother at about this time, particularly the distinction between 'venial' sins and 'mortal' sins. We'd been taught that venial sins were fairly far down the pecking order, minor offence type of thing. Telling little lies, for example, or having feelings of envy; using minor bad language. Venial sins were not hard to confess to in the confession box, but the mortal sins — these would do you in for sure. If you were not absolved from mortal sins, you were destined to spend eternity burning in the everlasting fires of Hell.

The Sisters did not try to shield us from this unpleasant fate. 'If you've ever suffered a little burn,' they told us, 'say from a candle or a spark from a fire, or perhaps a hot kettle, you know how powerful and painful that is. Now imagine that magnified, not ten or twenty times, not a hundred or a thousand times, but by a million times. And the pain goes on not for a moment, not for minutes or hours, or days or weeks, or months or years, but *forever* — and your misery is shared by other sinners all gnashing their teeth and writhing about on the Devil's pitchfork — well *that's* what hell is like.' How the Sisters knew so much about hell and the ramifications of mortal sin, I'm not sure, but I wasn't about to argue, in case arguing itself was a sin. What I did know was that if you clocked up ten venial sins, that counted as one mortal sin, and if you had the stain of mortal sin on your soul you could not go to Communion until you'd been to confession to wipe the slate clean again.

At college, Mass was at seven thirty every morning of the week, except on Sunday, when you got a sleep-in because it was at eight thirty. Although my sins were mainly of the venial variety — impure thoughts, lack of respect for teachers, etcetera — I'd accumulate enough each day to add up to at least one mortal sin. The guilt was incredible — I took this all very seriously. I couldn't bring myself to go to Communion in a state of mortal sin because that was an even greater sin, and of course the other kids noticed if you didn't go to Communion on a regular basis. I figured I must have been recognised far and wide for the sinful hopeless wretch I was. To make matters worse, everyone knew I was a trained altar boy, and this is where the business of 'testing God' came into it.

A couple of pagans and myself came up with a wickedly brilliant idea to confirm once and for all whether there really was a God or not, because if God really did exist, he was sure to strike us dead for the sacrilegious scheme we'd dreamt up. At Benediction on Friday evening, just as the host was presented to the congregation, we three altar boys would have a contest to see who could get the biggest stiffy. If there was a God, then it was a dead cert that at least one of us, if not all three, would end up a pile of smouldering cinders at the foot of the altar. The judges were to be the kids on the choir bench, off to the right hand side of the chapel, who had a bird's-eye view — just in case it came down to a photo finish.

I could hardly concentrate on the first part of the service, imagining that I was about to die a hideous death, followed of course by my passage into Hell. As the time approached, the three of us, with our eyes closed, must have seemed either in a state of total reverence, or distracted little buggers whose minds had wandered off elsewhere. I daresay the latter was more likely the case. I thought of all the rude things I could — Dusty Springfield was in there, as were parts of the actress Sabrina's anatomy. I knew I was doing well, and pulled my cassock tight to accentuate my 'development'. The other little cheats did the same, so I thrust my pelvis forward as far as I could and again, the others did the same. How we all didn't topple backwards down the steps I'll never know. What any observer must have thought of this carry-on was anyone's guess, and in spite of my best efforts I lost, and lived, vaguely disappointed on both counts.

Did we prove whether or not there was a God? Nobody was struck dead on the spot, but I still wasn't able to bring myself to go to Communion, just in case. The stain of mortal sin was still on my soul — and now I'd added considerably to it. Given my exploits, you'd think I took religion lightly, yet the guilt was real. It just seemed that the more terrible the sin might be, the greater the temptation was for me to actually commit it.

Religion certainly wasn't boring in those days, especially if you were blessed (or cursed) with an active imagination like mine. Novenas were an interesting innovation of the sixties. If you went through the ritual of attending Mass and saying special prayers for nine consecutive days, you were guaranteed entry to Heaven, even if you accidentally died in a state of sin. (I had to wonder who in their right mind would *deliberately* die in a state of sin.) Whoever it was that worked out this interesting piece of enterprise bargaining with God was never made clear to us, but those in authority said it was so, and therefore it must be so. In my school years I made at least three Novenas, so I figured that whatever I might get up to later, I should be fairly well covered.

Then there was Limbo. You don't hear too much about Limbo these days, unless you're talking about the Chubby Checker dance craze that followed hot on the heels of the Twist. This was another Limbo; it wasn't Heaven, it wasn't Hell and it wasn't Purgatory — it was something different altogether. For those without the benefit of a good Catholic education, the hierarchy of afterlife destinations went like this: top of the not to be contemplated category was Hell, where all sinners who died with the stain of mortal sin on their souls writhed around in agony for eternity while the Devil laughed his head off. It went without saying that if you went straight to Hell you'd be in the company of all the communists who ever died, and the likes of Lee Harvey Oswald and Adolf Hitler. Mr Khrushchev was sure to go there the moment he slipped off the perch too!

Moving from the pits upwards, we come to Purgatory; not as bad as Hell, but not good either. Purgatory seemed to be rather harder to explain, and depending on who you listened to, you got a slightly different version of what it might be. Generally speaking, you went to Purgatory if you'd been naughty, but not downright bad enough to go to Hell. Here you served out time until you were ready to go to Heaven. We prayed a lot for dead relatives who might be stuck in Purgatory. It was hard to say whether or not souls were tortured there; apparently the worst thing about Purgatory was that you could not look upon the face of God. As far as I could see, that wouldn't be such a bad thing, as long as you were comfortable. Frankly, I thought that when I died, I would probably know quite a lot of the people there. I suspected Arthur Calwell might end up in Purgatory, because Dad reckoned he wasn't 'all bad'!

Next up the ladder was the even more mysterious Limbo, the destination for babies who died before they were baptised. I was convinced our dogs Wallaroo and Tarpeena went there too. I couldn't bear to think that they just died and didn't go anywhere. Besides, they both had proper Catholic burials with holy water we nicked from the font at the entrance to the church. I don't know what this revealed about the existence of a soul in a dog, but we had been told by the nuns that Saint Teresa was such a good person and had led such a good life, that her body didn't decompose after she died, it remained 'incorrupt'. About a month after Tarpeena was killed we dug him up to have a look — clearly he hadn't led such a good life.

Also in Limbo were the non-Catholics, who just 'didn't know any better'. It used to worry me a bit, all those Catholic babies in Limbo being brought up by Proddies, until it dawned on me that half my relatives were Protestants, in fact apart from Damien, *all* the Cameron side were, including Mama Cameron and Aunty Jean, and they were perfectly lovely people. So perhaps Limbo wasn't so bad after all, and at least there'd be plenty of dogs.

Then we get to the top of the heap, the big one, Heaven. Available and welcoming to all who had led a perfect life. From the little I knew, I couldn't imagine the place would be over populated. Of course all the saints would be there, and the popes (we weren't taught about the bad popes — we only found out about them much later), as well as all the priests, the brothers and the nuns. The priests and the nuns I was sort of okay with, but the thought of sharing any time at all after death, let alone eternity, with the Marist Brothers was a bit daunting. Purgatory wasn't looking so bad after all — it was too late for Limbo as I'd been baptised when I was a baby. I remember the nuns telling us how wonderful Heaven was, and when I asked what people there did all day, I was told they were 'blissfully happy' because they could spend all their time 'looking upon the face of God' — frankly TV sounded more interesting.

* * * *

In September 1963 my Mama Harrap died after suffering a heart attack. I was at college and my brother Peter had to break the news to me, which could not have been easy for him. I thought I was going to die too. This was my first experience of a death close to me, and I didn't handle it at all well. Mama had lived at our house so often she was a very close part of the family. She was in her eighties and still extremely active, so I suppose it was good to go suddenly, however I couldn't console myself with that at the time.

Peter and I were allowed to go to her funeral. It was awful. I hated seeing the coffin being lowered into the ground. Afterwards all the older relatives went back to Aunty Elvie's for drinks, and apparently had a really good time. Mum said some of them acted little better than savages. For 'behaving like savages' read 'had a bit too much to drink'.

I knew for certain that Mama Harrap would have gone straight to Heaven. I was also positive that she could see everything that we got up to, and that even she would have thought we'd 'crossed the line' from time to time.

Perhaps as a result of Mama Harrap's sudden death, my mum went into early labour with Murray, the second youngest in the family, and he was born seven weeks premature in September 1963. Maybe that's why he was always the runt of the family, though a pretty fit runt at that.

When she was alive, Mama loved to go shopping. She'd take the bus to Melbourne for the Myer sales, which was quite an expedition. She'd dress up to the nines in very smart clothes, and wore a fur coat in the days when it was still respectable to have a dead animal draped over your shoulders. In Melbourne she'd go to the variety spectaculars put on by JC Williamson's. We knew all about the 'Follies' show she went to at the Tivoli Theatre, because she brought home a program which she kept in a drawer in her

Singer treadle sewing machine cabinet. The fascinating thing about this program was that it featured a page of chorus girls in feathers, with absolutely nothing covering their breasts. There they were, stark raving naked. When Mum found out we'd been looking at 'rude' pictures in Mama's room, she gave her a telling off. But Mama wasn't afraid of her. 'Melda,' she said, 'it's only nature.' Mama should have known all about 'nature', she'd had twelve kids.

When someone you really love dies, it's interesting the things you miss. I missed Mama terribly. I missed sitting up in bed with her and half a dozen other brothers and sisters on Sunday mornings. I missed the distinctive scent she always wore, and her tuneless singing of old songs — 'I don't love you anymoooore ... I won't holler down your rain barrel'; the way she let me put my head in her lap on long car trips and fiddled with my ears until I went to sleep.

Another devastating death at that time was the assassination of President Kennedy. It was a Saturday morning when the siren sounded, summoning all the boarders to assemble in the quadrangle. To be summoned on a Saturday morning usually meant we were going to have a busy bee of some kind or another, or that we were going on an excursion, perhaps to the beach, although usually that was planned much further ahead. For whatever reason, it was highly unusual for the siren to be blown on a Saturday morning. When the Principal delivered the bad news we were all in a state of shock. On top of the Cuban missile crisis, I'm sure everyone thought the Russians were behind the assassination. We went to the chapel straight away for a Mass for the dead President. Although I was only twelve, it seems like yesterday that we heard the news. I felt upset for the President's kids now they had lost their father, and I was worried about who would now stand between us and the Russians — all the stories about Russia were overwhelmingly negative.

* * * *

As if I didn't hate the college enough, school sports days were testing in every sense of the word for me. I was no athlete, so I loathed sports with a passion. I thought that sports days must be a bit like Purgatory on earth. There were four teams named Moorak, Lavalla, Tenison and Champagnat. I was in Lavalla, the yellow team, and competed among the lower divisions, except for the shot-put, where because of my size I was reasonably good — not terrific, but certainly better than I was in the track events. It was a pathetic sight to see my division on the track towards the end of the day. All the fat and uncoordinated kids lumbering around the Flat, gasping and wheezing and sweating profusely. Mum used to say it wasn't the ribbon that counted, but the fact that we put in the effort and had a go. Once I actually won a ribbon for coming second in something, whereupon I knew Mum's little homily was rubbish — I loved getting that ribbon. The fact that I had improved my handicap by deliberately running even slower than my usual slow pace in the heats was beside the point. One other kid at least had obviously used the same strategy — the one who came first!

Swimming was much fairer on the fat kids because we had built-in natural buoyancy. None of us were actually champion material, but at least we didn't sweat so much and the kids built like whippets didn't win everything. Like every other fair-sized town in Australia, Mount Gambier had an Olympic size swimming pool built shortly after the success of the Melbourne Olympics so that every kid might have the chance of emulating our Olympic heroes. The Mount Gambier pool was a couple of miles walk from the college. We'd go there most weekends in the warmer weather, and also for swimming carnivals. We had interschool carnivals with kids from the state schools, as well as from Monivae, a Christian Brothers college in Hamilton, not far across the border in Victoria. Like our showers, the swimming pool had a 'foot rot' bath you had to wade through before you could get in the water. And the canteen there sold giant biscuits for threepence. They were like Milk Arrowroot biscuits, only about six times the size; it was the only place I ever saw them.

Interschool carnivals extended in winter to football. Because he was so good at the game, 'Roo Dog' Yeates was invariably captain. Yes, Roo Yeates was one of the few kids from Our Lady of the Pines to go on to Marist Brothers, only now he was known as 'Roo Dog'. Because the college was so much bigger than the primary school in Nangwarry, I generally managed to keep out of Roo Dog's way. I was never picked in any of the footy sides, even in the lowest divisions, unless the captain wanted one of the other side's players 'hobbled'. I could usually manage that by 'accidentally' falling on them. If you placed your elbow really well, you could achieve a darn good winding, to ensure the target took no effective part in the game for at least ten minutes. Usually it also meant that I took no further part in the game, but that wasn't considered too much of a loss, by me or anyone else. Playing football during winter in

Mount Gambier was not one of life's great joys. It was invariably freezing cold and drizzling icy rain. Soaked to the skin, you just hoped the kids on boiler duty had done their job properly so that at least you could thaw out in the showers.

* * * *

There were some happy moments at Marist Brothers, even associated with sports, but they were very few and far between. Some of the better times were cross-country runs on the weekends, in my case more of a cross-country 'walk'. We'd set off from the front of the college and head up the side of the Sugar Loaf, then around the caldera to Browne's and Valley lakes, scaling Mount Gambier before coming back down through the oak forest alongside the Flats. Mainly, I tried to escape from my woes at college by immersing myself in a book. The best start to any book I ever read was the opening of *A Tale of Two Cities* by Charles Dickens: 'It was the best of times, it was the worst of times' — and that pretty much summed it up.

I think the reason I hated college so much was because I was basically a bit of a 'sooky' kid. I had spent the first eleven years of my life in a home full of warmth and love, surrounded by siblings and our hordes of extended family and friends. And, despite the fact there were so many of us kids, we were each allowed not to like one thing, mine being porridge. College was so much of a change from all this. Suddenly a cold draughty dormitory to sleep in, indifferent food eaten in a big, noisy refectory, classes four or five times the size I'd been used to, and the mainly stern and humourless brothers who contrasted so starkly from the kindness of the Brown Joeys.

I was only at the college for three years, but it seemed like a decade. Academically, I hit the wall, limping from first into second year, then repeating second year, at the end of which I was virtually 'invited' to leave school to save my parents the considerable amount of money it was costing them for negative results. I left school a month before my fifteenth birthday.

13

The Cheese Factory, 1966

I immediately applied for a job at the local newspaper, the *Border Watch*. The job was an apprenticeship as a typesetter. Mum reckoned that once I got my 'foot in the door' I could work my way up to become a journalist. The fact that twenty other kids with far better academic results were probably applying for the same job was beside the point. A few weeks went by and I got the knock-back from the *Border Watch*. I didn't even get as far as an interview. Dad said it was probably because the people who ran the *Border Watch* were Methodists, and they'd know I was a Catholic because I'd gone to Marist Brothers.

Peter was working at home with Dad on the farm, but I didn't want to be a farmer. Frankly, I didn't know what I wanted to be, all I knew was I wanted a job so I could make a bit of money and have some independence. Dad's youngest brother Allen was a cheese maker at the Glencoe West Cheese Factory, and a job came up there for a general 'dogsbody'. I was in. The factory was a few miles from home and I didn't have a driver's licence — I'd only just turned fifteen — so I boarded with an elderly retired couple. Mr Rees was a bit of a crotchety old thing but Mrs Rees was an extremely sweet woman, and their old stone house was dark and cool in the heat of summer. My room was a sleep-out on one side of the house. Mrs Rees used to make the most delicious bubble and squeak for breakfast, made up from the leftovers of the meal the night before. She'd do the fry-up in an old heavy-based pan with lashings of butter, and made toast on a hand-twisted wire fork in front of the coals in the old Metters stove.

Mr Rees had an old-fashioned cylinder wind-up phonograph, the like of which I'd never seen before. It had a huge trumpet for a loudspeaker. It was terribly scratchy to listen to, but I was fascinated by it. It was light years from the state of the art Philips Mum and Dad had at home. The Reeses also had a big old-fashioned valve radio on which we would listen to the ABC seven o'clock news and perhaps a serial if we were lucky. Mr Rees was very much in control of the radio. With one of my first pay packets I bought myself a second-hand television, an old grey vinyl covered thing in a metal cabinet. It fizzed and crackled in damp weather. The Reeses were quite shocked. They didn't approve of television, and my rent was increased because they had the idea that it used up an enormous amount of electricity. Mrs Rees used to come in to say goodnight sometimes, and would sit on the side of my bed watching TV as long as she dared. I think she would have loved one of her own.

I was at the Reeses' in the months leading up to the fourteenth of February 1966, when we were bombarded on TV and radio with the jingle announcing the introduction of decimal currency — 'In come the dollars and in come the cents, out go the pounds and the shillings and the pence' — to the tune of 'Click Go the Shears'. When the new currency first came on the scene, everyone was fascinated by it. The new one dollar note was roughly the same colour as the old ten bob note, and the two dollar note was similar to the old one pound note, but they all looked a bit like play money.

Glencoe is a very pretty place, with gently rolling hills and flats, generally surrounded by pine forests. The soil is dark and rich and ideal for dairying. On winter mornings, the frost would often lay thick on the ground, giving the appearance of a snowfall. As you walked on the grass, it would crunch and break under your feet like tiny shards of glass. It was so still on frosty mornings and evenings that the smoke from the chimneys of the houses and milking sheds would rise straight up into the sky. Sometimes just before dark someone would be playing bagpipes — I could never tell exactly where the sound was coming from, but you could almost imagine you were on a Highland moor.

The cheese factory was quite old. It had a huge boiler into which we'd stoke pine offcuts. They'd burn extremely rapidly, so it was a never-ending job to keep the boiler fed. The milk was pumped into a row of huge stainless steel vats, the culture added, and the cheese-making process begun. It was always hot in the factory, even on the coldest days, and we'd swelter in our heavy overalls and rubber boots. Splashes of milk and whey would get down into the boots and combine with sweat, so that by the end of the day they were fairly potent. We'd have to sluice them out with water, and hang them up-side down in the boiler room to dry out for the next day, to start all over again.

They were mainly older blokes working at the factory, although there was another kid just a bit older than myself called Doug. He had a grey Morris Oxford, not the coolest car on the road, but a car nonetheless. Doug often gave me a ride to work in his Morris; it was massive inside and pretty much indestructible. Because Doug and I were the juniors, we got to do all the menial jobs, like scrubbing out the huge stainless steel cheese vats and packing the big blocks of cheese. The work was mindless, and there was plenty of time to think about the mess I'd got myself into. I certainly didn't want to spend the rest of my life in a cheese factory, doing all the crappy jobs.

The recurring line in my report cards kept coming back to haunt me: 'Has the ability but lacks the application.' Boy did I wish I'd applied myself. Before things went terribly wrong at Marist Brothers, I'd wanted to be a school teacher, like Sister Andrina. I just knew I could teach kids to like reading and learning like she did. I wondered if anything could be worse than working in the cheese factory. I thought not.

The up-side of having a job of course, even a crappy job in a cheese factory, was the money. It paid bugger all, but it was better than nothing. After paying my board, there was still enough to buy Coke and other rotgut, and to go to the drive-in on the weekends. It didn't really matter what the movies were, and we sat through some shockers, *The Music Man* being memorable amongst them. The drive-in was the place to be on Saturday night, especially for a newly employed fifteen-year-old whose brother was old enough to be driving a car. Charles and Malcolm would often come too, and we'd deck ourselves out in our Rolling Stones boat-necked shirts, tight jeans and pointy toed shoes and head for the bright lights of Millicent, about fifteen miles away. Four teenagers crammed into a Mini is a feat at the best of times. When all those kids are six feet tall or more, it's a downright miracle.

Millicent wasn't a very big town, but at least it had a drive-in. I don't remember its name, but it seems every drive-in of the time was called 'Something-Line'. Mount Gambier had the Starline, and elsewhere were the Moon-Line and the Sky-Line. They sprang up all over the place, even though the south-east of South Australia was not the ideal locale for a drive-in, especially in the winter months, which seemed to be most of the year. If it wasn't raining cats and dogs, you'd be fogged in so badly you'd be lucky to see the car in front of you, let alone the screen.

There were all sorts of stories about how to clear fogged up windows, but nothing really worked. A towel just left lint all over the screen. Tissues came to bits too easily and made a hell of a mess. Some bright spark heard that a freshly cut potato rubbed over the windscreen did the trick. Well, it did stop the misting to a certain extent, but you ended up with a screen so smeary you couldn't see anything anyhow. Then came the little tin bar things with rubber suction cups and a heating element in them. You stuck these to the inside of the windscreen and plugged them into the cigarette lighter. They were quite effective for demisting about one square foot of windscreen, but that was hardly enough for all of us to peer through. Worse, they'd run the car battery flat in a very short time. Not that flat batteries were such a major problem though, because there were always plenty of bodies about to do a push start. Some flash kids even had jumper leads, though they were mainly the kids who borrowed their dad's car. And if you've ever spent much time looking for the battery in a Mini, you'd realise the jumper leads wouldn't have been of much use anyway — in the early models, the battery was cleverly disguised under the rubber mat in the boot of the car.

There was a certain degree of drive-in etiquette you were expected to observe. If the car in front of you hadn't put its aerial down, for instance, you were entitled to flash your headlights at them until they did. One night this resulted in some tough Millicent kids ('common as muck' as Mum would say) coming back to our car and smearing a choc-ice all over the windscreen. Apart from being a waste of a perfectly good choc-ice, the greasy smears were virtually impossible to get off given the limited resources available at the drive-in loo. But the toughs who did the smearing hadn't reckoned on the four Cameron boys, and the bastardry they were capable of when roused. We bought a large bottle of Coke from the canteen and shook it up vigorously as we were leaving the drive-in after the show. Driving slowly past the toughs' car we sprayed it with Coke from bumper to bumper. If you've ever sprayed sixties duco with Coke you'll know it does wonders!

* * * *

A Mini 850 was not the fastest car on the road in those days, but what it lacked in straight line speed and pick up, it more than made up for in manoeuvrability. Going for a drag was a favourite pastime, and something we often did after the drive-in. The process began at the Commercial Street lights in Mount Gambier, leering at the kids in the car alongside, then taking off as fast as you could when the lights turned green. Invariably we'd be left in the dust of the average Holden or Vauxhall or Austin, however if we followed the smart-arses who won the initial drag, it wasn't too difficult to coax them into giving chase with face pulling, impolite finger gestures or, in desperation, a darn good mooning.

Once we'd provoked someone in a more powerful car to give chase — and they always did, they fell for it every time — Peter and his Mini came into their own. We'd buzz off up the side of the Mount and into the pine forest behind the Blue Lake, the suckers in hot pursuit. The forest was crisscrossed with tracks and firebreaks, and apart from the wider firebreaks, most of the tracks were winding and narrow, with barely enough room for even a tiny vehicle to pass between the trees. It was ideal for the Mini, especially when the driver knew the lie of the land as Peter did. Any pursuers could be given the slip in a few minutes. If someone was really persistent and had a reasonably small car, for example a hotted up Cortina, Peter would head straight for the rim of the volcano, above Valley Lake and behind the hospital. Here, there was a walking path with white posts blocking vehicular access. We'd open the front windows of the Mini and clip back the side mirrors to narrow the tiny car even more, then belt between the white posts with barely an inch to spare on either side. It did your heart good to watch the pursuers screech to a halt or, if they weren't quick enough, do some fancy remodelling to the front of their vehicles.

* * * *

The red and white Microbus was not a cool vehicle to do the drags in, and when Dad finally decided to trade it in on another car, the heavy duty nagging really started. He eventually narrowed his choice down to a couple of Chev Belairs. One was a green and white six-cylinder model for sale at OG Roberts, the Holden dealers in Mount Gambier. It was about a 1959 model, quite spectacular, with twin headlights and gigantic fins. The other was at the Carlin and Gazzard yard. Dad took us all into town one evening to have a look at them. The green and white Chev was by far the biggest car at the OG Roberts yard, and it was certainly beautiful. But then we went to Carlin and Gazzard. In pride of place, up on the stand under the spotlights, was a V8 Chev with a white top over a mushroomy pink body. It was a year newer than the green and white one and its fins were slightly more subdued than the earlier model, but not so much that it mattered; they were still enormous. The bodywork gleamed under the spotlights and the acres of chrome reflected the myriad lights shining down on it. It had red leather upholstery and I knew I'd die if Dad didn't buy it.

Dad, however, was leaning dangerously towards the green and white car. He and Mum were discussing it at length on the way home: the six-cylinder would be cheaper to run, being an earlier model it was cheaper anyway, etcetera. We threw in our tuppence-worth about the V8 being newer, and that the bigger motor would be better for towing stuff around the farm. Dad decided he'd go back to town the next day and see who'd do the best deal; then he'd make his mind up.

The rev head in him prevailed, thank God, and he went for the V8. It was just too gorgeous to be true. It had plush maroon carpet and I sat for ages in it when he brought it home, smelling the leather seats and gazing in awe at the space age dashboard and the metal binnacles which protruded out over the instrument panel. The binnacles were a bit like the sails of the Sydney Opera House. I suppose the idea was to shield the instruments from glare, but like all American car design in those days, they were definitely more flair than function. In a crash they would have been lethal, but then, cars like this didn't crash did they? The speedo, as I pointed out to anyone who'd listen, was marked up to one hundred and forty miles per hour!

But the real joy was the outside. Chevs in Australia, as the sales bloke pointed out, had their bodies made in Canada by the Fisher company, and were far superior to the United States-built ones. I had to agree, the Belair was beautifully put together. It had twin headlights of course, and a grille that must have kept the chrome-plating factory busy for weeks. The windscreen was massive and curved right around the sides of the car, the boot lid was like the flight deck of an aircraft carrier, and the fins were the most wonderful fins you've ever seen. Not overstated and garish like the fins on Dodges and Chryslers, but more flattened and stylish. Under the fins, and surrounded by more acreage of chrome plating, were the brake and indicator lights, a whole bank of them on each side.

When we went to town in the Belair, and especially on those rare occasions when the car wasn't overcrowded with babies and toddlers, I thought I was Lord Muck. Elbow casually resting on the wide windowsill, I assumed the pose of one for whom it was the most normal thing in the world to be swanning around in the most supremely divine vehicle under God's sun. If a kid from school happened to notice us, as they often did, I'd adopt an air of, 'Oh, this old thing.' From now on, there would be no more humiliation at the lights on the main corner, no more ducking between the white posts to evade pursuers. We'd be the kings of Commercial Street — if we could only prise the keys off Dad.

At the start it was impossible to get Dad to give us the Chev. We'd plead and entreat, nag and downright grovel, but to no avail. Eventually Peter managed to persuade him to let us take it to the drive-in. By now he had traded his Mini for an XP Falcon ute (much more practical for farming purposes), and though it had a wide bench seat, four kids was definitely stretching it. It was worse than the Mini. But finally having possession of the Chev keys, why would you waste a perfectly good Saturday night sitting at the drive-in where so few people could perv on the car? We skipped the drive-in altogether, and did laps of Commercial Street, soaking up all the admiring glances until it was time for the drags.

From then on, this became our pattern, and I'm sure we used more rubber in a night than Dad would in a month of normal driving. The down-side was the cost of the petrol; the Chev was a thirsty beast, especially with a leadfoot at the wheel, and you couldn't return the car with an empty tank, because then Dad would know for sure what we'd been up to. But gradually the Saturday night drags became less interesting, as more and more kids arrived on the scene with their dads' X2 Holdens and Super Pursuit Falcons, and by that time the novelty of the Belair had begun to wear off anyway.

14

Going West

With the family rapidly growing up, Mum and Dad had some big decisions to make. The dairy farm was doing okay, but it was not big enough to support a number of families, and the folks assumed that with six sons, at least some of us would be interested in continuing on the farm. Peter, who was now seventeen, had no particular girlfriend yet, and we no longer had Mama Harrap, so if a decision was to be made about a major upheaval, then now was probably the time. But where? Land in South Australia's south-east, which had been settled since the previous century, was fairly expensive. Each week Mum and Dad would pore over the property pages of the *Weekly Times*. It seemed that the more settled areas of Victoria and New South Wales were just as expensive as the south-east. By comparison, land in more far flung places in Australia was now being opened up for development and appeared to be far better value.

Gradually Dad narrowed down the areas of interest to the Atherton Tableland in far north Queensland, and the south-west of Western Australia. Many a discussion took place at night about the price of

Family Christmas get-together and farewell at the Glencoe Hall. Mum and Dad in the middle, baby Imelda on Mum's knee, then clockwise from left: Bernadette, Josephine, Malcolm, Charles, me, Peter, Gerard, Mary and Murray.

land in the west and in Queensland, two areas, funnily enough, at the very opposite corners of the country. We knew a little about the west. My cousin Damien's family had moved to Kojonup in Western Australia a couple of years before, and his dad, Uncle Neil, had written to my dad with glowing reports. There were also stories from other South Australian farmers who had moved to the country being opened up around Esperance and discovered that, with the addition of trace elements to the soil, what had appeared to be 'hungry' and 'gutless' country could not only be made productive, but could positively thrive. Altogether, the south-west looked interesting, and it seemed the best thing to do was to go and check it out.

With the full complement of ten kids, it took some organising, but finally Mum and Dad flew to Perth from Adelaide in a Whispering T-Jet, taking Imelda the baby, who was still being breastfed. With Uncle Neil they looked at farms throughout the Great Southern region. They didn't settle on a particular property, but had soon decided they'd seen enough to convince them the West was the place to go. The moment they arrived home they set about arranging the sale of the farm and all our things in readiness for a new life in Western Australia. To us kids, the West seemed like the far side of the moon, but it was all terribly exciting.

Beanbri sold quickly, and we had a clearing sale to get rid of all the stock and machinery, as well as the furniture and household items that were just too impractical to take with us. Sadly, most of the library went, packed up in boxes and sold as job lots. I packed the books myself, and it was like saying goodbye to old friends — some of them easier to farewell than others. The kids' books I'd long outgrown, but I was just getting into Hammond Innes and Alistair MacLean. I sat high on the roof of the homestead and watched the auctioneers down at the cattle yard as they sold off the stock. There was heaps of household stuff laid out on the old overgrown tennis court at the side of the house. Mum and various relatives were kept busy making tea, cakes and sandwiches for everyone. It was a fairly sad day.

Once the farm was sold and cleared, it didn't take us long to gear up for the trip. In readiness for the big move, Dad bought a red ex-PMG Austin truck at a government auction. Peter of course had his Falcon ute, with a trailer hitched to it carrying a 240-volt, twin-cylinder Lister diesel generator, which was to provide our electricity in the West. The fact that we would have to generate our own electricity spooked us a bit — just how primitive was this place the folks were taking us to?

On the back of the Austin truck, Dad fitted a metal stock crate, which he covered with a thick green tarpaulin. Here was packed all the bedding and personal belongings we could jam in. The back of Peter's ute was stuffed with cases and clothes, and the Chev, with a sixteen-foot caravan hitched behind, was packed with kids. All the vehicles would travel in convoy. The trek west was going to be quite an ordeal; the road across the Nullarbor was not yet sealed, and it was the height of summer. Uncle Jock, one of Dad's younger brothers, had volunteered to help with the trip, so now we had four drivers between the three vehicles. Mum had the baby Imelda to look after, so Peter did most of the driving in the Chev, while Dad and Uncle Jock took turnabout in the ute and the truck.

In the days immediately before we left, there was a constant procession of friends and relatives calling around to say goodbye. It was hardest of all saying goodbye to Robin and his mum and dad, Aunty Iris and Uncle Glen. They were like my second family. I said I'd be back to visit often, not quite realising just how far away Western Australia was. The furthest I'd ever travelled was Adelaide, and that seemed to take forever.

The morning we set off from Beanbri was very sad. More family came to see us off, and there were plenty of tears all around. Aunty Maureen had made a cake for my sixteenth birthday, which was just a couple of days away. Given that Aunty Maureen had seven kids of her own, I was amazed she even remembered it was my birthday, close as it was to Christmas.

For the last time we passed between the beautiful ornamental trees that lined the driveway at Beanbri. The day was already beginning to warm up and the hot dry wind from the north made a mournful sound as it roared through the needles of the cypresses. It was a relief to get on the road, even though our progress was painfully slow. The ute and the truck had to crawl through the Adelaide hills, showing signs of overheating, it was such a hot day. The Chev, even though it was dragging the cumbersome old caravan, was breezing along.

At the end of day one of our journey, tempers were a bit frayed. Everyone was hot and bothered and Mum was particularly snappy. It didn't pay to look at her sideways. No doubt the basic logistics of keeping ten demanding kids — including a baby and toddlers — fed, cleaned and clothed under fairly primitive circumstances explained her dark mood somewhat. We stopped that first night at a caravan park at Clare and it was great to get out of the hot vehicles, stretch our legs and have a shower.

It looked like more scorching conditions were on the way from the west, and Mum and Dad were keeping a close eye on the weather forecast. They decided that henceforth we'd travel at night if need be, and rest up somewhere shady during the day. Ceduna, virtually the last town in South Australia before the desert, was right on the coast, and they thought if we could make it there in the next couple of days, we could wait out the heat for a cool change, then cross the Nullarbor as quickly as possible.

We set off early the next day, and already it was stinking hot. There had been some thought about stopping in Port Augusta, but it was sweltering there, so we decided we might as well press on towards Ceduna for a while. This was my sixteenth birthday. Had we been staying in South Australia, this was the day I could have gone for my driver's licence. In Western Australia you couldn't get your licence until you were seventeen. Just my luck! It had even passed through my mind that our move to the West was just a ploy to delay me getting my driver's licence. Now that's paranoia! Mum's mood remained brittle all day, so it paid not to ask for anything.

As soon as the sun started to go down and it began to cool, we pulled off the road into a disused gravel pit just outside the town of Wudinna. Mum soon had a huge saucepan of baked beans heating on the tiny gas stove in the caravan. Uncle Jock had a flagon of port which he'd stashed somewhere in the load; it was covered in dust, but a couple of swigs out of that and he was happy. Some birthday, I thought. But after stomachs were filled and calm had started to descend on the camp, we cut Aunty Maureen's cake and everyone sang 'Happy Birthday' to me, so it didn't turn out quite so bad after all.

As night fell we were easily able to pick up radio stations all over Australia and we were anxious to hear a kids' station in the West. At last we found 6KY in Perth. They were counting down their top ten, which was promising because most of the songs we were familiar with, in fact they were almost identical to the Adelaide charts. Then came the shock — the number one record in South

Australia was Ike and Tina Turner's 'River Deep Mountain High', which was pretty cool. When they got to the number one record in Western Australia, it was the theme from 'The Trap', played by the Ron Goodwin Orchestra — what kind of backwater were we headed for?

My sleeping spot was the back seat of the Chev, which wasn't too bad really since the car was so big. If it got a bit too cramped or hot, I could just hang my feet out the door, as long as I jammed something against the button to stop the interior light going on. Once the baby and little kids were fast asleep, Mum calmed down considerably, and just as the rest of us were getting drowsy she became quite amiable and chatty. It was a really clear night. Away from the lights of civilisation the sky was inky black with a mass of stars strewn across it. All we wanted to do was sleep, but then Mum started spotting satellites. I'd just start to nod off when she'd come and shake my foot. 'Quick, come and look at the satellites, they're so easy to see. See how many you can count. I can see at least four.' Mum was very excited about it all.

That night of my sixteenth birthday, I swear I almost used the 'f' word!

First published 2003 by
FREMANTLE ARTS CENTRE PRESS
25 Quarry Street, Fremantle
(PO Box 158, North Fremantle 6159)
Western Australia.
www.facp.iinet.net.au

Reprinted 2003.
Copyright © Eoin Cameron, 2003.

Consultant Editor Janet Blagg.
Production Coordinator Cate Sutherland.
Cover Designer Marion Duke.
Typeset by Fremantle Arts Centre Press.
Printed by Griffin Press.

National Library of Australia
Cataloguing-in-publication data

Cameron, Eoin, 1951– .
Rolling into the world: memoirs of a ratbag child.

ISBN 1 920731 06 7.

1. Cameron, Eoin, 1951 — Childhood and youth.
2. Legislators — Australia — Biography. I. Title.

328.94092

The State of Western Australia has made an investment in this project through ArtsWA in association with the Lotteries Commission.